AF560392

RE-IMAGING JOBS IN A FAST-CHANGING WORLD

Also by the author

The Economic Reactor

RE-IMAGING JOBS IN A FAST-CHANGING WORLD

Rajiv Bahl

RUPA

Published by
Rupa Publications India Pvt. Ltd 2021
7/16, Ansari Road, Daryaganj
New Delhi 110002

Sales centres:
Allahabad Bengaluru Chennai
Hyderabad Jaipur Kathmandu
Kolkata Mumbai

ISBN: 978-93-5333-536-6

Second impression 2021

10 9 8 7 6 5 4 3 2

Printed at Saurabh Printers Pvt. Ltd.

Jodi Keu Kôtha Na Kôe, Ore Ore Ôbhaga, Keu Kôtha Na Kôe
Jodi Shôbai Thake Mukh Firaee Shôbai Kôre Bhôe
O Tui Mukh Fute Tor Moner Kôtha Êkla Bôlo Re

(If all keep their mouths shut, O my unlucky friend, if no one dares speak
And everyone turns their faces the other way in fear,
You alone speak out your mind freely, as loud as you can)

—An excerpt from Rabindranath Tagore's
'*Êkla Chôlo Re*', which has always motivated me.

CONTENTS

PROLOGUE

I started writing this book in the beginning of 2019. It was to be a book written leisurely, a project I enjoyed working on and researching for. Having long been a science and science fiction fan, it was fascinating to read about all the technological breakthroughs happening in almost every field. Many of the science fiction fantasies that thrilled me in my boyhood years were set to become reality. Flying cars were already flying and if Elon Musk had his way, trips to Mars would be commonplace. There was virtually no area where technological innovations were not disrupting the traditional way of doing things. Many solutions that were hitherto not possible were becoming inevitable. It was apparent that in the future, machines powered by artificial intelligence, would be doing more and more of the work that was now being done by humans.

By the end of 2019, it was apparent that, with increasing automation in many fields, jobs were eventually going to be lost to artificial intelligence (AI) and robotics. There was, however, no panic, either among the general population or governments worldwide. The entire process of automation and job losses was expected to take place over a period stretching over two to three decades, by which time surely, the job market would find its own equilibrium. Many predicted that while some jobs were likely to be lost, other jobs would be created. They cited the Industrial Revolution, when millions of jobs had been lost in farming but many more created in other sectors. Indeed, the thinking among experts and governments was about ways of retraining people, who were laid off, to do other jobs. Not many entertained the possibility that there would be few jobs left for humans to train for.

There was another reason why governments the world over were sanguine about the way things were going. At the end of 2019, equity markets across the world were at or near all-time highs. Companies were making more profits than ever before. It was easy to ignore the fact that companies were producing more and making more profit with fewer and fewer people. Governments, especially elected governments, are more focused on the present than on problems that may arise a couple of decades in the future. Even if the extent of the coming job losses is fully visualized, the tendency is to leave those issues to be sorted out by future governments.

I, on my part, had been researching the coming changes in different fields, for over a year, and was beginning to realize the extent of both the plenitude that would be created by the technological breakthroughs, as also the unavoidability of job losses in the not-too-distant future. Having cheap and abundant goods of good quality can never be a problem. Having no jobs and hence, no money to buy these goods is certainly a problem. Yet these two outcomes, namely cheap and abundant goods on one hand and no jobs to earn the money to buy them with on the other, seemed to be the likely consequences, no matter which area I looked at. I set about thinking if this particular circle could be squared. Could we have both—the abundance and the money to partake of that abundance?

The problem is not completely intractable. As I was mulling over this conundrum, one solution presented itself. It was not a conventional solution and it was also daring to boot. I was not electrified. It would require too much courage to implement it. Still, I kept tossing it about in my mind and trying to iron out the wrinkles, as I perceived them. It was more an exercise born out of curiosity than anything else, much as I would try to solve a Rubik's Cube—something I am rather bad at. There was no sense of urgency. I, like everyone else, considered the coming loss of jobs to be an event that would occur sometime in the future. Technology was moving in the direction of human job losses. It was moving at its own pace. Innovation was changing our lives, one step at a time.

Then the virus from Wuhan hit the world and the luxury of time was gone. Jobs started being lost by the millions the world over, including India. The extent as also the speed of the job losses was unprecedented. It did not take people long to realize that many of the lost jobs would not be coming back. Companies are beginning to realize that they can make do with fewer people. The adoption of AI technologies and automation is speeding up. It is almost as if the coronavirus has pushed the fast-forward button for job losses. The job losses that had been estimated to take place a couple of decades from now, will probably be upon us in less than a decade. The start of this acceleration is there before all of us, to see and understand.

There have been pandemics and other calamities earlier. Mankind has experienced volcanic eruptions, tsunamis, ice ages, droughts and floods and other pandemics before now. These were random punches thrown at us and we coped with them the best we could. We had no control over these events, nor any shield against them. These events were termed to be acts of God, neither caused nor solved by us.

The pandemic caused by the coronavirus is different on two counts. The first is the origin of the virus and the possible cure for it. We do not, as yet, know definitively if the virus jumped from another species to humans through a random mutation, or if it was created in a laboratory and escaped accidentally or even if it was released purposely in what could be construed as an act of war. Maybe one day, we will know for sure. The cure for the virus and the creation of a vaccine against it is within our reach. It depends on us how soon we are able to do that. Possibly the origin of the virus and certainly the cure for it are in the hands of man and cannot be thought of as acts of God. At the time of the Spanish flu pandemic a century ago, we did not possess the ability to either create a virus or cure it.

The second big difference between the time of the Spanish flu and now is that at the time of the Spanish flu, there were no technological advancements waiting in the wings, ready to enable us to do things differently. Once the deprivations caused by the Spanish flu were over, there was no alternative, but to limp back to the old ways. That is not the case now. In order to survive, businesses are shifting to digital solutions and automated production lines, precluding the possibility of employment returning to pre-virus times.

According to the McKinsey Global Survey results of June 2020, the vast majority of respondents to the survey expect unemployment rates in their countries to rise further in the coming months—39 per cent expect the size of their workforce to decline over the next six months. This is the highest share to say so since April 2009. Half the companies will accelerate their adoption of business technologies, such as digitization, AI and automation.[1] This will ensure that even after the virus is controlled, jobs will keep reducing. The first part of this book gives a very good indication of the areas and extent of job losses that can be expected.

The effects of the coronavirus have already been devastating and the virus is still raging. The figures, as at the end of November 2020, make for grim reading and are continuing to rise. Worldwide, nearly 60 million people have been infected with the virus, 1.4 million have died from it, and close to a billion jobs have been lost.[2]

Governments across the world are trying everything they can think of to ease the pain of the situation. The printing presses are being fired up and incredible amounts of money are figuratively being printed. All thoughts of fiscal prudence and deficit spending limits have been given the go-by. The American government has pumped in about USD 5 trillion into the economy by way of loans at near zero interest rates and by subsidies. That is about a quarter of the American GDP. The UK government had launched the 'Eat Out to Help Out' plan, pledging a 50 per cent discount to restaurants, cafés, pub or eligible food service establishments. The 50 per cent discount was to be covered by the government for the full month of August 2020.[3] These are panic-bordering responses in an attempt to kick-start their economies and are clearly not sustainable in the long run.

There is as yet no coherent long-term plan that recognizes the tectonic shift that has taken place in our lives. The shift is permanent. If a vaccine that neutralizes the threat of infection from the virus is found by the end of the year, as many predict, things will not go back to the old normal. The new normal that will emerge will be very different. Supply chains will shorten. Manufacturing will get more automated and more local. Meetings, both business and social, will increasingly be on screens rather than face to face. Hydrocarbons will be replaced by solar and wind energy. World trade patterns will change. Most importantly, jobs will greatly reduce.

I realized that the book I was working on dealt to a large extent with the phenomenon of reducing jobs and what could be done to counter its debilitating effects. Only the time frame had shrunk, from about a decade or two, to the here and now. I also felt that I had a workable solution, which was sustainable for the long run. It is a different matter whether any government or other decision makers see merit in what I have to say. For me, the time for dawdling over the book was over. I now had to get the book out where it could be seen, read, discussed and perhaps, acted upon.

I realize that what I advocate in this book is not the normal response to financial crises and job losses. It will also require political will and political courage. There is an old English proverb, 'Cometh the hour, cometh the man'. It means that no matter what the situation, a person will appear who can turn the tide and win the situation. In this case, it could be an individual or a government. In India, we have all grown up with the concept of an avatar, which means nearly the same thing.

As an Indian, I can only hope that the saviour will appear in India.

INTRODUCTION

We are living in a period of great change. This was not always so. We emerged as a species in Africa about 200,000 years ago. As we spread out across the globe, aided and hampered in turns by ice ages, warmer periods and supervolcanic eruptions, there was not much change in either our knowledge base or our practices. It took us, as a species, about 135,000 years to invent the bow and arrow. For nearly 190,000 years or about 95 per cent of our existence, we were all hunter-gatherers before we learned to farm. It took us another 5,000 years before we invented writing. After that, change speeded up a little. Even so, for thousands of years, there was little to differentiate between the lives of any set of grandparents and grandchildren.

Compared with those many millennia of imperceptibly slow, almost glacial change, the rate of change over the past few hundred years can only be described as frenetic and increasing. Until we stop to think about it, we seldom realize that most of the objects and experiences that impinge upon our lives did not exist a mere 300 years ago. Then there were no steamships, railways, automobiles, airplanes, electricity, radios, televisions, refrigerators, canned food, telephones or photographs. Transport on water was by sailing ships or hand-poled barges. On land, it was by animal-driven carts, wagons and chariots. Or it could have been by human-powered rickshaws and palanquins. Our wheels did not have tyres. Air-filled tyres are less than 200 years old and were made for the then newly invented bicycles.

In 1969, I met a charming, ninety-year-old lady in Long Beach, California. She was lucid and revelled in narrating her life experiences. As a little girl, she remembered moving with her family to California in a covered wagon train and she had, in her life-time, seen on live TV the first men walking on the moon. 'All in a lifetime' as she repeatedly emphasized. She remembered seeing her first electric bulb, her first automobile and following in the papers, the activities of the Wright brothers. In 1969, she was particularly excited about the new Jumbo jets that could have carried her entire school twice over, with room to spare. She was not alone in experiencing this great pace of change. All of us who are, let us say, forty years of age or older, can point to quite a few things that we experienced for the first time, which did not exist ever before.

We, as a species, started out experiencing little or no change for tens of thousands of years. Then gradually, change started coming into our lives, slowly at first but then, with increasing frequency. Now change is upon us at a breakneck speed. Barely a year passes without a few developments taking place that have the potential to change our lives in major ways. The amazing part of it is that new discoveries and developments are happening in not one, or even a few fields of endeavour, but across almost all areas. We seem to be living inside an explosion of change.

The little girl travelling to California in a covered wagon train in the late 1880s did not know it, but Thomas Edison was then busy perfecting the light bulb. Marie Curie would not discover radioactivity for another ten years and the Wright brothers wouldn't take off for another fifteen. Karl Benz had just built the first car and the Ford Model T was twenty years into the future. Radio waves were yet to be discovered and Guglielmo Marconi was still to make the first radio communication. Charles Darwin had propounded his theory of evolution, but the existence of genes would not be accepted for another fifteen years and the discovery of the DNA molecule was sixty years into the future.

Small, apparently innocuous discoveries or events can yield stunning results, unimaginable at the time. Karl Benz could not have imagined that his experiments with a horseless carriage would put the world on wheels. Neither could Marie Curie have thought that her observation of some sort of rays being emitted by lumps of uranium and thorium would lead to nuclear power plants and thermonuclear bombs. No one watching the first flights at Kitty Hawk could have visualized Jumbo jets, supersonic flights or lunar landings. Thomas Edison's incandescent light bulb was at first regarded as a parlour trick or curiosity, but it changed the very texture and time frames of our lives, opening up the night for us. Marconi could not have conceived the thought that his radio waves would lead to hundreds of channels of real time television, all in living colour. The monk Gregor Mendel, who had failed in every teaching job he attempted and was busy growing and observing pea plants in the corner of a remote monastery, could not have thought that his work would lead to recombinant DNA molecules (DNA molecules constructed in the laboratory by genetic recombination), giving us the power to create new life forms, a job hitherto reserved for God.

All the above examples progressed from first experiments to world-changing phenomena in less than fifty years. There are other such examples, such as the discovery and development of antibiotics and high-yielding crops. Today, we are at a point where not only are new discoveries being made every month in diverse fields, but many of these discoveries have moved on to experimentation and even beyond, to first implementation. Significant advances have been made in the fields of automation, AI, renewable alternative energy, medical diagnosis and treatment and many other areas. There is more progress being made across many fields right now than at any other time in the history of our species. Surely, not all discoveries will lead to successful products and practices. But many will.

We would be naïve to assume that these new developments, taken together, will not impact our lives in as profound a manner as did electricity, automobiles and air travel, to name just three. Some of the coming technologies may even have the potential to alter our lives as significantly as did the Industrial Revolution itself, which changed the world from a largely pastoral and farming one to today's largely urban, manufacturing and services-oriented world.

This is not a book claiming to look into the future. I am not Nostradamus. Of all the incipient technologies being currently experimented with, some will be successful and others not. Of the ones that are successful, some will have wider acceptance, depending on the benefits they deliver, whereas others will have only a marginal impact. It is difficult to pick up any one emerging technology in its nascent stage and predict with confidence, the impact it will have upon our lives. It is easier to imagine the impact on our lives of technologies that have already matured from ideas to experimentation to initial implementation and met with some success.

We know that solar cells, wind turbines, robots and AI, to name a few, have already begun changing our world and are here to stay. The only thing debatable about these technologies is, how soon and to what extent, they will be used. Self-driving cars and trucks are also a reality and their widespread usage is inevitable. The time frame for their roll-out is a little more uncertain. Other emerging technologies, such as designer babies, tweaked to be resistant to many diseases, with greater life expectancies, are more difficult to predict. Apart from technological hurdles, they also face ethical and safety concerns. These concerns also hold true of some ventures like depleted uranium community-size power plants, which use the residual and depleted fuel from existing reactors, and cultured meat grown in a petri dish. We must keep in mind, however, that if the underlying know-how exists, what is either not practical or acceptable to do today may suddenly be imperative to do because of changed circumstances or developments in other fields.

Regardless of what happens to any particular idea or emerging technology, the broad contours of change are unmistakable. Unless there is a complete break down of the world order that ushers us back into another Dark Age, it is apparent that not only is great change upon us, it is also accelerating.

Whether and to what extent a technology is accepted depends mainly on the benefit it delivers to users of existing processes. It does not depend as much on the pros and cons of existing technology. The Stone Age ended not because we ran out of stones but because better alternatives were discovered. Coal mines and cars with internal combustion engines will come to an end not so much because they are polluting the environment but because better and cheaper alternatives are now available. The more benefits that a new alternative can deliver, the quicker and more widespread will be its acceptance and the quicker older solutions will be abandoned. Solar energy is already competing with fossil fuels. If following Moore's Law, the price of solar panels is halved or efficiency doubled, there would be few open terraces, anywhere in the world, that are not colonized by solar panels. For this to happen, it will not need vast public outlays of money. Companies and individuals acting in their own interests will ensure a quick switchover.

This book is divided into two parts. The first part looks at the changes happening across diverse fields. I do not think that a single book can cover all the new developments taking place on an almost daily basis and the resultant changes to our lives that these developments are unleashing. The changes are too many and evolving too quickly to chronicle them all. Furthermore, discoveries in one area often trigger new breakthroughs in quite different areas. An area of great promise is the interplay between computers, AI and medicine or the biological sciences as a whole. As I write this, newspapers are carrying the story of a newly invented and marketed device. It is a handheld ultrasound machine that is operated through a smartphone. The doctor testing the device discovered a 3-centimetre cancerous growth in his own throat, which he did not know of earlier. Coupled with

AI, which will also interpret the images, this one device alone has the potential to shift many diagnostic tests from the doctor's clinic to the home, speeding up diagnosis and hence, treatment.

While it may not be possible to chronicle all evolving breakthroughs, this book focuses on a few fields of endeavour that are responsible for a great number of jobs. Apart from the effect on jobs, their impact on the environment and economic growth have also been examined.

The source material for tracking the many developments and breakthroughs that are taking place in varied fields is varied. It ranges from books to newspaper articles to newsletters and to follow-up searches on the web. At the time of writing, I have tried to be as up-to-date as possible. I have also narrowed my field of enquiry to just a few developing trends that I think will have the most profound effect on our lives. Despite limiting myself and being diligent in my research, I am certain that anyone who researches the same topics a few months from now, will come across more breakthroughs in at least some of these areas. This is not a shortcoming on my part but reflects the rapidity of change. Having said that, I must add that the more newer developments take place, the faster will be the coming of a changed world that is headed our way.

How soon will these changes come? Let me answer that question from a personal perspective. I am seventy years of age and I expect to see many of the things this book discusses become reality during my life. My children, who are approaching middle age, will in their lifetimes see more changes than this book can foretell. It would be presumptuous for us to think that entirely new breakthroughs that take us by surprise will not continue to happen. The world that my grandchildren inhabit, when they are grown up, will be alien to me. Were I to step into that world, I would be more disoriented than Rip Van Winkle ever was!

Will the world of my grandchildren be a better and happier one than the one I have known, or will it be horrendous instead?

That is what this book is about. With change comes opportunity. We should seize the opportunity and in the words of Omar Khayyam, remould the world nearer to the heart's desire.

First, however, let us peer into the future. Peering into the future is not devoid of surprises. The path to the future is neither predetermined nor smooth. Very promising endeavours can suddenly be thrown out of kilter because of completely unforeseen developments, including those of a technological, political or economic nature.

The Iridium satellite constellation is one such example. It was conceived in the early 1990s as a constellation of seventy-seven satellites in order to provide voice and data coverage to satellite phones, pagers and integrated transceivers all over the globe. The satellites were deployed between 1997 and 2002 at a then cost of USD 5 billion. There was much excitement and anticipation the world over. For the first time ever, a person anywhere on the planet could directly call another person anywhere else in the world. Then along came cell phones.

Cell phones had been completely unanticipated when Iridium was conceived. Cell phones could deliver the same services to all the populated parts of the world at a fraction of the cost. Iridium lost the bulk of its potential customers and went bankrupt. It was the largest bankruptcy in US history till then. After the bankruptcy, a new entity emerged to operate the satellites and it now caters to a limited clientele, which includes explorers, journalists, military units and also terrorists.

The point to note here is that at times when a promising technology does not work out, it may be because a still better alternative is now available. This can only speed up change.

Sometimes a very promising technology can be stopped in its tracks by a seemingly unsurmountable problem. In the year 2004, scientists discovered and created in the laboratory, a new allotrope of carbon and called it graphene. It has near magical properties. It is 200 times stronger than steel, a ten times better conductor than copper, totally transparent yet impermeable to all gases, very flexible and could make the fastest semiconductors. Its discovery generated immense excitement with possible uses ranging from quantum computers to a stairway to space and from super-efficient lighting to cheap desalination of seawater. There was one problem though. No one knew how to make it in any sizable quantity. Many ways were tried but none were successful. The interest started ebbing, but tenacious scientists kept trying. Then in 2019, a trio of scientists from the University of Cambridge claimed to have solved the problem. They spun off a company called Paragraf to manufacture graphene and promised to market the first product using graphene later that year. They have not yet disclosed what that product will be.

Should the claims of Paragraf hold true, there is no way of telling in how many ways our world will be changed from how it is now. Various new endeavours are happening in many other fields with varying degrees of promise that also include nuclear fusion power plants which have, for the first time, started attracting private money. However, these are still at a very nascent stage and I have not considered them for the purposes of this book. By pointing these out, I only wish to emphasize that the developments considered in this book are not exhaustive. Change is coming to us from more directions than it is possible to imagine, and it is coming fast.

It is possible that these coming changes, taken together, will have consequences that go beyond jobs, the environment and growth. They may tell upon our very evolution as a species. There are only some pointers towards this last, but they give rise to some unsettling thoughts, which I feel I must share. I have done so at the beginning of the second part of this book.

We cannot put the genie of knowledge and innovation back in the bottle. We cannot stem the pace of new ideas and discoveries. We must try and harness this flow of discoveries so that it leads to more rewarding lives for the vast majority of our citizens rather than giving way to chaos and the breakdown of civil society, which disruptive changes are equally capable of causing.

The main worry about AI, automation and all the other changes that we see approaching us is jobs. If AI and automated machines are going to do everything for us, what will we do? Optimists say we need not worry about jobs. Jobs, they aver, will not vanish but only shift from one sector of the economy to another. The only thing, they contend, we need to focus on is retraining people to do other jobs. They point out that a whole army of people will be needed to write programs and algorithms and also to design and manufacture hardware, including sensors and other equipment for specific tasks. Ignoring the fact that many of these processes will themselves become more automated with passing time, we can agree that a whole army will be needed for these new tasks.

The trouble is that while we may need an army of workers for these new jobs, we are going to put many other armies out of jobs. I refer to the armies of drivers, shop floor workers, workers in fast-food outlets and any other job that is repetitive and common enough to be worthwhile to automate. That will only be the start. Wherever pattern recognition matters, such as medical diagnosis, AI will outperform humans.

Optimists, who think that the total number of jobs will not decrease and may even increase, often point to the Industrial Revolution. They contend that while there was a major displacement of populations and agrarian jobs greatly diminished, the total number of jobs increased greatly; the same thing will happen this time around also. I find this argument to be specious for two reasons. The first is that there is no guarantee that every revolution or major upheaval in human affairs will always have the same results. The second is that the avowed purpose of the Industrial Revolution, if ever it was openly admitted, was to make things cheaply by replacing muscle with mechanical force. With low living standards and consequently, low wages at the start of the revolution, employers found it economical to employ many people to work in tandem with machines. Large companies often employed tens of thousands of workers and the very large, over a hundred thousand. Their number of employees was a matter of pride for them. With rising wages, the focus shifted to making do with fewer employees. With the blooming of AI and automation, we now seem to have crossed a tipping point. The avowed purpose of businesses now is to have as few employees as possible. Estimates put the extent of current jobs that are vulnerable to automation at between 40 to 50 per cent of all jobs. I doubt that as many new jobs can be created by the automation industry. We will have to look elsewhere.

There is a growing body of literature, of a doomsday nature, where, because of AI and automated processes, humans are replaced by machines of one kind or another and become largely unemployable, resulting in redundancy and poverty for the vast majority and the concentration of wealth in the hands of a very few. This outcome is certainly a possibility, but so are other happier outcomes. We need to be sagacious in the choices we make in the very near future.

The time to make the choices is now. Self-driving cars and trucks will start appearing on the roads of some countries in the next couple of years. By 2030, they will be mainstream there and will have made inroads in other countries. The factories that make the cars and everything else will have more machines and fewer humans. Jobs will not vanish at the flip of a switch. It will be a gradual process as more and more AI and robotics enter manufacturing plants. The process has already started and will keep speeding up. By 2025, general conversations the world over will refer to the ongoing job losses. By 2030, the same conversations will have a hue of panic in them. What we will all need to do at that point is to avoid being complacent and stop believing it to be a passing phase and that things will soon revert to the normal. There will be no normal to go back to. No amount of tweaking of interest rates by central banks will matter. The changes coming our way will be too strong to be controlled by such palliative measures. We will have to reorganize our society and the ways in which we interact with each other until we find a new normal, hopefully a happier one. As long as we are broken up into countries, acting more or less independent of each other, some countries will find a happier normal than others. Some will come to it sooner and some perhaps not find it at all.

The second part of the book looks at the things we can do both individually and collectively to cope with the coming changes. As individuals, we can do little more than keep ourselves informed about all the changes taking place around us and be aware of the jobs that can be taken over by AI or robots or machines in general and position ourselves accordingly. The role of governments in coping with the coming changes is much greater.

Governments will literally have to plant, nurture and grow another parallel economy focused on job creation, with limited scope for machine participation, to function alongside the existing economy. This is not impossible. It is probably much easier than it may at first appear. To set up the new parallel economy, governmental effort will be needed mainly on three fronts. First, is starting an unconditional Universal Supplementary Income scheme. Second, is on the ease of doing business with a focus on starting new business ventures. Constraints in doing business arise mainly because of bureaucratic processes. It will not be enough to remove some of the constraints. A complete reorientation of governmental and bureaucratic thinking is needed. Their stance will have to reverse from hampering to actively speeding up the start of new ventures. With the right incentives, this reversal of orientation can be made to happen. Third, is writing a new tax code for the new parallel economy. The prioritization for the new parallel economy has to shift from government revenues to the creation of jobs. Absurdities such as treating angel investments as taxable profits must be put down with a heavy hand.

Handled properly, this new parallel economy has the potential of creating, in India alone, 60 million new jobs in a couple of years.

Let us step into the future, the not-so-distant future.

PART ONE

OUR CHANGING WORLD

1

ARTIFICIAL INTELLIGENCE

I have two grandsons, aged seven and four, in whose esteem I have recently fallen. They have discovered that their all-knowing Grandpa is not really all that smart. He does not know much about superheroes at all and still has the quaint belief that Superman is the greatest superhero of all. They magnanimously conceded that Superman may have been a great hero once upon a time but today, every crook in the galaxy knows about Kryptonite, both red and green, so Superman is not so powerful today.

With infinite patience, they explained to me that it was all about powers and which superpowers a superhero had. The Atom, for example, could shrink himself to a microscopic size and still have his full weight. Upon my stupidly enquiring as to how that was possible, I was given a very special kind of look and explained how easy that was. All that the Atom needed to do was squeeze out all the empty space between the atoms of his body. I will refrain from going into the powers of the other superheroes for the fear of getting it all wrong and falling further in their esteem.

After licking my wounds for a while, I decided to hit back with a superhero of my own. This superhero, I explained to them, was not a storybook hero but a real one. When asked about his powers, I said he has many powers. For starters, if he looks at you once, he knows everything about you—your name, when you were born, your school, your class and your girlfriend's name. It also knows about every time you did not finish your homework. This got their interest. I was able to tell them more about the new superhero which, of course, is artificial intelligence or AI until they lost interest a few minutes later.

However, this got me looking at AI in a new way. If it is all about powers, AI is well on its way to becoming a superhero. Rather, it is on its way to make superheroes out of all of us and at the same time, also changing the world around us in more ways than we can imagine.

It is difficult to overstate the impact AI will have upon us. Of all the breakthroughs and discoveries taking place around us, AI is the game changer. It is the force multiplier. It has the potential to make every machine ever made into a sentient machine for some purpose. It will blur the difference between the animate and the inanimate.

AI is not to be visualized as something residing in banks of supercomputers, churning out solutions to the world's problems, although science fiction writers have sometimes pictured it as such and depending on the writer's inclinations, it has been seen either as a benevolent presence leading to peace and prosperity or a malevolent one, intent upon taking over the world. AI, as it is developing, will be far more pervasive, embedded in the most advanced as well as the most ordinary of gadgets.

AI, like human intelligence, is dependent on three factors:

1. The brain or hardware for computational ability.
2. Our senses or sensors to gather information and data.
3. Learning or algorithms to act upon the data gathered.

1. The biological brain has been evolving for millions of years, long before Homo sapiens appeared on the earth. The start of AI may be put at 1974 when the first widely used microprocessors or Central Processing Units (CPUs) arrived on the scene.[1] These CPUs led to multiple CPUs on a single chip, to Graphic Processing Units[2] (GPUs) capable of parallel processing of information, speeding up their capability by hundreds of times, to stacked GPUs mimicking the neural network of our brains. The latest development is the

announcement in May 2016 of a Tensor Processing Unit (TPU) by Google. Google has stated that TPUs were used in the AlphaGo versus Lee Sedol series of man-machine Go games, as well as in the AlphaZero system which produced Chess, Shogi and Go playing programs from the game rules alone and went on to beat the leading programs in those games, without being further programmed. The program taught itself by playing against itself in a matter of hours. An individual TPU can process over a 100 million photos a day.[3]

The evolution of AI has been over a million times faster than the evolution of our brains and there is no reason to believe that this rapid evolution will stop any time soon. Even at the stage where it now is, AI can do some things better than any human. It makes the humble calculator calculate faster and more accurately than any human. Or drive cars better and safer. Or a myriad other things we are in the process of discovering.

2. Our senses are the apertures through which we experience the world around us. AI uses sensors for perceiving our world. As far as our senses go, they are not particularly good apertures.

We perceive light with our eyes and label what we can see as visible light. Visible light is part of the electromagnetic spectrum. The electromagnetic spectrum ranges from Gamma rays with wavelengths of about 1 picometre or a trillionth of a metre or smaller than the size of an atom to Extremely Low Frequency (ELF) waves, with wavelengths of about a hundred thousand kilometres. Our eyes can see only a very miniscule portion of the total spectrum and it ranges from violet starting at a wavelength of 380 nanometres to red at 740 nanometres. If we compare our visible spectrum to the entire electromagnetic spectrum, we are very nearly blind. Our instruments and sensors and thereby, AI can view the entire spectrum.

It is the same with our other senses. Our ears can hear sound frequencies from 20 hertz to 20,000 hertz. We cannot hear sounds below 20 hertz or infrasound. Neither can we hear sounds above 20,000 hertz or ultrasound. AI can hear more than us. Ditto for the sense of touch. A proximity sensor can detect an object even before it is touched. A touch sensor can measure and control the pressure of the touch to a fraction of a millibar. As for the sense of taste, sensors are going well beyond what we can do. An Israeli start-up by the name of 'Consumer Physics' has come up with a device which, when pointed at, for example, a food article, can give a breakdown of its chemical make-up, along with a break-up of proteins, fats and carbohydrates. It can do a food analysis for meats, dairy products, fish, chocolates, fruits and vegetables, among other things, all displayed on your smartphone. It is in effect a molecular sensor or a spectrometer. It is like giving ourselves a sixth sense. And six is not a final number.

There are sensors that can sense direction, pinpoint your location on the planet, measure temperature, take professional quality pictures without an array of expensive lenses and yet more sensors with many other abilities. The list is long and increasing. As far as sensory perceptions go, sensors on which AI works have gone well beyond what millions of years of evolution have given us. One sense on which our sensors have not improved upon is our sense of smell. Not much work has been done on the sense of smell. But that is changing. A great deal of focused research is being done on olfactory science, or the science of smell, with a view to making it a powerful tool for the diagnosis of disease. I will come back to it in the chapter on health.

Some of the things that tiny sensors do today could only be done with expensive bulky machines earlier. Benchtop spectrometers could only be found in major laboratories and cost around USD 50,000. The smartphone-sized one that Consumer Physics makes, sells for about USD 250 with the price likely to drop. Expensive and bulky gyroscopic compasses and high-end photographic equipment come practically free, embedded in smartphones. The price of sensors is already low and dropping further. The average cost of a sensor is estimated to be 38 US cents by the year 2020.[4] This dramatic cheapening and miniaturization of sensors and computing chips will make AI ubiquitous. AI will be embedded in the most expensive and the cheapest of objects. Its uses will range from the profound to the frivolous.

There is another source of information input available to AI. It is the Internet of Things (IoT). IoT is the extension of Internet connectivity into physical devices and everyday objects. Embedded with electronics, Internet connectivity and sensors, these devices can communicate and interact with other such devices over the Internet and they can be remotely informed, guided, monitored and if necessary, controlled. We humans too can access the Internet. We need to log on to it through a device and then access whatever information we desire. With IoT, the information and data available on the Internet impinges directly upon the awareness (perhaps a debatable choice of word) of the gadget imbedded with AI, much as we perceive light and sound. This is yet another sense that we humans do not possess. The advantages are significant and difficult to fully imagine. When self-driven cars become the norm, each such car will be informed about the next course of action of all other vehicles in the vicinity. (This time I have avoided using the words 'aware' and 'intent'). Road accidents will be a thing of the past, along with human drivers.

3. The output of the sensors goes to a computer chip doing the work of a CPU which, to put it simply, is the brain of the device in which AI has been embedded. Depending upon the complexity of the work to be done, the chip can range from a low-end CPU to a high-end stacked GPU or a TPU. GPUs are hundred times faster than CPUs and TPUs faster still. General purpose stacked GPUs are being used in training Deep Learning neural networks and TPUs are used in programs that teach themselves to play chess or work better than the best earlier programs in a matter

of hours. TPUs speed up machine learning.

In humans, once the information from the senses reaches the brain and depending on the knowledge already stored in the brain, the brain determines its next course of action. A human baby starts acquiring knowledge from birth. First through its senses, then as it begins to understand language, through the spoken word, teachers, the written word and any other means which are accessible to it. This is a process that takes years before a human can function more or less independently.

AI is never a babe in the woods. It is manufactured with much of what it needs to function in the designated role embedded in it. You don't need to teach a calculator to calculate. A new self-driving car will not need to be taught traffic rules afresh. In addition to being pre-programmed, each artifice embedded with AI and connected with others like it through the IoT is constantly updating its knowledge base and helping other such units do the same.

Once the signals from the various sensors embedded in a device reaches the CPU, it determines what is to be done. This is possible because of instructions programmed into the CPU. These programs are referred to as algorithms. An algorithm is a set of instructions for performing a specific task or calculation or data processing, leading to what can be called automated reasoning. An algorithm may be a relatively simple one, such as telling a lamp to switch on once a light sensor indicates that brightness has fallen below a certain level. An algorithm can also be very complex as in face recognition technology, where inputs from a visual sensor are used to identify one human face from possibly billions of faces. In fact, AI cannot only identify individuals, it can also read their emotions in real time.

How can AI do all this? The answer is data. It is Big Data and superfast processing that makes it all possible. For face recognition, AI is shown millions of pictures of people and it measures and stores the shapes and sizes of facial features, such as the shapes and sizes of different noses, eyes, lips, ears, chins, hair patterns, skin colours, cheeks, moles, warts and everything else. When a face recognition camera sees you, it measures all your features instantly and if given a name, can recognize you again anywhere. If not given a name, it will still be able to recognize you and link that up to every time and place where you have been seen.[5] This is at least as accurate as fingerprints are for identifying people. As far as emotions are concerned, there is no intuitive or deductive reasoning involved on the part of AI. It is shown millions of pictures of happy faces, confused faces, anxious faces, frightened faces, worried faces and so on. AI then recognizes what happy faces, sad faces and so on look like. If put out at a street crossing, an AI camera, which has access to all this data, can say with certainty that Harry, Hans, Hari or Harriet passed this way going north, looking very harried.

This capability immediately brings to mind concerns about Big Brother or a police state. However, the technology is neutral. It can just as easily be used to identify a confused student in a large class needing special attention or identifying a runaway child at a bus or railway station or identify a depressed person roaming the streets. I daresay that a human can identify these same situations too, but AI is on the job every second of every minute of the day and never gets distracted. Have you ever seen somebody and struggled to remember the name or even if it was someone you knew? AI is never wracked by these lapses of memory. Indeed, when you travel outside your country, your definitive identity is not confirmed by an immigration officer comparing your face with the picture in your passport. It is now established by the AI-enabled camera that you are directed to look at. If you visit a country without these cameras, you can be certain that the country has some catching up to do as far as AI is concerned.

Self-driving cars have driven for millions of miles, mainly in the western part of the US with accident rates far lower than for human drivers. Critics contend that the comparison is unfair. The automated cars have driven mainly on one way, clearly marked lanes mostly in good weather and have not driven in all sorts of conditions that humans have been driving their cars in. The criticism in my opinion is valid. However, it is nobody's contention that automated cars have reached the zenith of their evolution and are today as good as they are ever going to be. It would be instructive to compare the performance of automated cars today to where it was five years ago and then try to visualize where it might be five years into the future.

This is true of every application of AI. Perhaps the most important thing to keep in mind about AI is that it can learn. If an automated car is involved in an accident, the events leading to the accident are analysed, the lessons are learnt, and corrective algorithms are installed to prevent such accidents from being repeated. The new algorithms are installed in all automated cars. Every car will not need to repeat the same accident to learn the same lesson. The same, unfortunately, cannot be said for human drivers. This gives us an idea about how rapidly we can expect further improvements in the performance of automated cars or indeed of any equipment that is powered by AI.

The process of educating AI is known as Machine Learning. In the example of how AI is shown pictures of happy faces, sad faces and so on, resulting in AI's ability to recognize the emotional state of a face in real time, is known as Supervised Learning. In the example of AI being shown features of different faces so that it can, on its own, devise the measurements of the different features of any new face it encounters, enabling recognition, is known as Unsupervised Learning. In the case of the self-driving car that meets with an accident and leads to a change in its operating algorithms, it is known as Feedback Learning, the accident in this case being the feedback.

With Machine Learning, new algorithms being developed and an avalanche of data becoming available to it daily, we will look back five years from now and be amused at how primitive AI was. What is this avalanche of data about? It is about you, about me and about everything under the sun.

Every time you order something online or browse the net, you create a data point. If you pay with your credit or debit card, you create another data point. If your car is fitted with the new smart number plates, every time a toll is deducted from your account or you pass an appropriate sensor, you create yet more data points. When you order a book, from say Amazon, you get recommendations for other books. Assuming your reading habits are a little different from mine, the recommendations I get will be quite different from the ones you get. The more books you order the more data is created about your reading preferences and the closer are their recommendations to your tastes.

AI does this with predictive algorithms like K-Nearest Neighbor Algorithm. The books you have read earlier are stored as data points on different matrixes, by subject, author, style of writing and so on. It also correlates with the books chosen by those who have reading habits similar to yours. A book that generates data points closest to your earlier choices is recommended to you.

My wife is a member of a Ladies' Book Club. She frequently asks me to order books for her. The books her club suggests she read, are completely different from what I like to read. There is hardly any common book. I order her books from my account. The reading recommendations I get fall into two distinct patterns. I can tell at a glance if a particular book is meant for her or for me. I do not tell her about these recommendations and wait. Sooner or later she asks me to order one or more of the books that have been recommended.

If our actions can be predicted with increasing accuracy, does it mean that free will is illusory? Are we more creatures of habit than we think we are? These are questions for philosophers to answer. Artificial intelligence will force philosophers to grapple with many other questions too. They will need to relook at privacy and property laws and will have to redefine sentient and non-sentient life forms.

It is difficult at this point in time to determine what AI will be capable of a decade hence. AI is currently in its infancy and acquiring capabilities faster than any human infant has ever done. Prima facie there will be little that AI and the machines and gadgets embedded with it will not be able to do better than any human. Most of us accept at some intuitive level that AI and machines will be able to do some jobs better than us, perhaps in manufacturing or even driving cars. Are we ready to accept that in the not-too-distant future, there will only be a very few tasks that we will be able to do as well as AI?

I recently watched on YouTube a few pieces of music composed by AIVA.[6] AIVA is the acronym for Artificial Intelligence Virtual Artist. AIVA recently became the first AI program to be recognized as a composer by a music society, the Society of Authors, Composers and Publishers of Music (SACEM). I am no music critic, but it sounded good to me. It was music written by AI and played by a human orchestra. AIVA is not the only AI program capable of creating music, there are others too. AI has the ability, after listening to the works of various composers, to create music in the style of say a Bach or a Mozart or a Hemant Kumar. We may one day get to hear a new Beethoven symphony which Beethoven never wrote. I doubt there are many human composers who would attempt to write an entirely new symphony as if written by Ludwig van Beethoven. The same is true of painting too. AI has started creating new art, both abstract and representational. Given a picture, it can recreate it as a surreal art piece as if done by Pablo Picasso.

There are few tasks that AI will not be able to do better and cheaper than humans can do. Before completing this chapter, I would like to conduct a thought experiment about coffee baristas, both human and AI powered. Imagine the AI powered machine having face recognition capability and be connected to the net through the IoT. It will know the time of day and the ambient weather.

There are two main varieties of commercially used coffee beans. Robusta beans have high caffeine content and make stronger coffee. Arabica beans have more flavonoids and give a richer aroma. When you walk up to an AI powered coffee machine for the first time, it will scan your face, file it away and ask your name. If you ask for say a cappuccino, it will give you one just like any other coffee machine. It will, however, have a simple feedback panel. It will enquire about your last cup of coffee for just three parameters—strength, aroma and cream. For each, you will have to punch one of three buttons—Okay, More or Less. The same choices will be given when you have a latte, espresso or a cold coffee.

The machine will remember this and make the needed adjustments in your next cup of coffee after which you can make further adjustments if you so require. The next time you visit the machine it will greet you by name, make your improved coffee and be ready to receive any further suggestions. After a few visits, it will know exactly how you like your coffee and if you prefer a stronger brew in the morning and a more aromatic one in the afternoon or the other way around. It will know how you like your espresso when you choose to have one. It will also know if, on a hot day, you prefer to have an iced latte and the way you like it. In a sense it will know more about your coffee tastes than you are aware of them yourself.

Because the coffee machine is connected to the IoT, every other coffee machine in the world will have the same information, either because it belongs to the same chain or through a customer information sharing agreement. If you and I walked up to a coffee machine in a new place, we would each be greeted by name and if we both ordered a cappuccino, we would be given our perfect brews even if our cappuccinos tasted very different from each other's. No human barista could match this. Coffee shops would no longer be able to compete on the quality of their coffee, as each coffee shop would offer the perfect brew to each customer. They would need to compete on hospitality and entertainment.

Coffee machines are very ordinary, commonplace things, which we more or less take for granted. They hardly seem to be the subjects for exploring the possibilities of artificial intelligence. That is the point. With its cheap sensors and processing chips, there will indeed be only a few artefacts that are not coupled with AI. Your shoes could not only tell you how far and how fast you have walked and the calories you have burnt, they could also tell you if there is a microbial build up in your shoes and if you need to air, wash or fumigate them. AI will be ubiquitous. It will be as readily available as electricity is today. Manufacturers of all sorts of devices will easily be able to enhance the functioning of their devices with easy AI solutions.

The more complex the machine or the task at hand, the greater will be the scope of AI to replace humans and as we have seen with the coffee machine, the more is the potential of AI to enhance the performance of the operation to levels that are not possible for humans alone to do. Within a few years, it will be technically feasible for AI to do most of the things that humans do today and even improve upon human performance. It may not be economically feasible to do so. Many quick service restaurant jobs will be replaced by machines, simply because it will be worthwhile to develop hardware and software for tasks with a huge demand. Fine dining and gourmet cooking jobs, or jobs involving specific local tastes will be more difficult to replace by machines as there will not be sufficient demand to justify the expense of automating the process.

As AI-aided automation takes over more and more tasks that humans do today, from factory floor jobs to driving cars and trucks and everything in between, there will be less for humans to do. Jobs will certainly be lost. The loss of jobs cannot be wished away or legislated against. The benefits that AI-aided automation delivers are too many to be ignored. There is an old saying that you cannot shout against thunder or words to that effect. Apart from goods and services of a better quality being delivered to customers at a lower cost, lives will also be saved. In India alone, there are 150,000 lives lost every year to road accidents. With automated cars and trucks, it is likely that deaths can be reduced to a tenth of what they are. Rather than trying to prevent the spread and evolution of AI, we should look at other avenues for creating employment and generating incomes in the hands of everyone.

The effect of AI on our lives will be profound. It will affect our jobs, our environment, the economy and the very fabric of our society. Little of this will be direct. Much as when electricity affected us greatly, it was through the devices and practices it enabled. In the following chapters, each of which focuses on different areas, I have tried to estimate the changes that will come because of developments in that area and tried to them all up in the final chapter of the first part of the book.

Sundar Pichai is the chief executive officer (CEO) of Alphabet Inc., which owns Google. Pichai was earlier the CEO of Google. Google is perhaps the leading company in the world working on AI. Pichai most likely understands the potential of AI better than most of us. It is interesting to contemplate on what he said about AI in an interview at the World Economic Forum gathering in Davos, Switzerland in January 2020. 'AI is one of the most profound things we're working on as humanity. It's more profound than fire or electricity.'[7] More profound than fire—it is humanity's first technological achievement that started differentiating us from the apes!

By the time my grandsons grow up to be young men, they will have realized that AI is indeed the greatest superhero of all. Its superpower is to be able to change the world in the blink of an eye in civilizational time frames. We must endeavour to ensure that the change is for the better.

2

ENERGY

The story of energy is changing again. It has done so a few times in the past. At the dawn of civilization, energy was human muscle power and biofuels, which we then called firewood, dry leaves, animal droppings or anything else we could burn like animal fat and beeswax. We used these biofuels mainly to cook and to warm ourselves and for a little light. Then we learnt to harness animals and added motive power to our uses of energy in the form of horses, carts, wagons and draught animals to till our fields. It continued to be this way for many millennia. Along the way, we took baby steps towards using other forms of energy by way of windmills and watermills, for either grinding grains or pumping water. We also put sails on our boats. We did not have a great deal of energy, nor did we have many uses for it.

Then along came the Industrial Revolution, with the steam engine to power it and coal to run the steam engines. The age of fossil fuels started. At first, coal was king. It powered all the machines that were run on steam. It powered the locomotives that pulled trains across continents and the ships that spanned the oceans. When Edison made the incandescent light bulb and electricity started to be generated, it was again in coal-fired electricity plants. With the invention of the internal combustion engine and the manufacture of automobiles, a need for liquid fuel arose and oil started becoming a major component of our total energy use.

After the Second World War, the ensuing peace and the

availability of electricity in homes caused a plethora of electrically operated labour-saving devices to be invented exponentially, from washing machines to electric toothbrushes. This caused a further demand for energy in the form of electricity. Industries too, where they could, shifted from steam to electricity. It was far easier to get an electricity connection than to set up boilers and steam pipes. Now, with the advent of electric vehicles, the shift from petroleum as a direct fuel to electricity will speed up.

Electricity is the new king. Electricity is also the great equalizer. It does not matter from which primary energy source the electricity is generated. It could be nuclear, hydroelectric, solar, wind, tidal or geothermal. The only thing that matters is the cost of that energy. If that energy is clean, it is an added bonus.

The demand for energy is increasing the world over. The greatest demand for that energy is in the form of electricity. Fortunately, so are the ways by which we can meet that demand cheaper than ever before. The cheaper new energy sources also do not contribute to greenhouse gases or pollution in general.

The three new sources are a new type of nuclear power plant, solar photovoltaic cells and wind turbines. Both solar cells and wind turbines have been around for some time, but the technological breakthroughs taking place in these two areas are so profound that it will completely alter the composition of our energy basket. Both solar and wind power are intermittent, there being no solar power generated at night or on cloudy days and no wind power when the wind does not blow. For these periods, we also need to look closely at power storage batteries.

Many of the technological breakthroughs that I speak of are very recent. Some of these are in the process of being implemented for the first time as I write this book. The developments I speculate upon have been validated in laboratories and in small-scale field trials. None of them are the results of wishful thinking. The only uncertainty is about the exact time of the roll-out of all these developments to complete the full cycle from energy generation to storage and to end use.

Until about ten years ago, there was a well-established and fairly stable energy basket and energy usage cycle. In broad strokes, it could be described as electricity being generated mainly by the means of coal-burning power plants, nuclear power plants, hydroelectric plants and later, natural gas power plants. Fuel for all transportation needs and electricity in a few remote locations came from oil. Solar, wind, biofuels, tidal energy and geothermal energy were all bit players in the energy basket. That is still true today, but change, quite rapid change, has started. The rapid growth of wind power started in about 2005 when the total world output was 59 GWh (Gigawatt hours or billion watt hours). In 2020, it is forecast to be 722 GWh—a growth of twelve times in fifteen years. Solar power generation took off in 2010 when world output was 40 GWh. In 2020, it is expected to be 850 GWh—a growth of twenty times in ten years.[1]

To understand the reason for the phenomenal growth of solar and wind power, a glance at the Table below will suffice. It is a Levelized Cost of Energy (LCOE) for 2019. LCOE is a term used by economists when comparing different technologies. The LCOE represents the total cost to build and operate a new power plant over its life, divided to equal annual payments and amortized over expected annual electricity generation. It reflects all the costs, including initial capital, return on investment, continuous operation, fuel and maintenance as well as the time required to build a plant and its expected lifetime. It also takes into account carbon capture and sequestration (CCS).

Below is a table giving the LCOE cost of 1 kWh of electricity in US cents.[2]

LCOE COST COMPARISON OF ENERGY SOURCES, 2019

Power Plant Type	*Cost in US cents per kWh*
Coal with CCS	12–13
Natural Gas	4.3
Natural Gas with CCS	7.5
Nuclear	9.3
Wind Onshore	3.7
Wind Offshore	10.6
Solar PV	3.8
Solar Thermal	16.7
Geothermal	3.7
Biomass	9.2
Hydro	3.9

This Table compares the US average LCOE cost for both non-renewable and alternative fuels in NEW power plants, based on US Energy Information Agency (EIA) statistics and analysis from Annual Energy Outlook 2019 (data for coal and combined cycles with CCS are taken from 2018 report). The emphasis on NEW is mine. The Table does not reflect the cost of energy from power facilities that are already up and running.

In August 2019, the Los Angeles Department of Water and Power signed a power purchase agreement (PPA) for solar power at 1.997 US cents per kWh and power storage at 1.3 cents per kWh. The deal is for a 400 MW solar and 800 MWh of storage for twenty-five years, slated to begin service in April 2023.[3]

GEOTHERMAL ENERGY: This is the energy in the form of heat lying below the earth's surface. It is inexhaustible, non-polluting, and accessible around the clock and only 3–8 kilometres away from any place on earth. Once tapped, the energy is free. The only drawback is that we do not yet know how to tap it in any significant measure. The only geothermal energy we can currently extract is from near the edges of tectonic plates as the heat there is near ground level.

One day, we may be able to easily tap into the vast amounts of energy readily available near us, but it is not likely to be soon.

TIDAL ENERGY: This is the energy that causes high tides and low tides twice a day. The obvious limitation of tidal energy is that it is limited to coastal areas. Not all coastal areas are suitable for extracting the energy of the rise and fall of the tides. A great deal depends on the underwater topography of the seabed to cause the rise and fall of water levels to be converted into a flow of water, which can be tapped to generate electricity.

While the energy of tidal flows is free to us, harnessing the energy is relatively expensive. Most tidal energy projects are dependent on government subsidies to be viable. There are a few places like Scotland where tidal power contributes significantly to the local electricity supply.[4] However overall, tidal energy is unlikely to contribute meaningfully to worldwide electricity supply.

HYDROELECTRICITY: This is a major source of electricity generation. Its fuel is free, clean and renewable. Hydropower generates about 16 per cent of the world's total electricity.[5] The cost of hydroelectricity is relatively low at between three to five US cents per kWh.

There is still a great potential to increase the production of electricity from hydropower. According to the International Energy Agency, 'The technical potential for hydropower development is much greater than the actual production.'[6]

This clean, relatively cheap power is increasing rapidly. According to the Hydropower Status Report issued by the International Hydropower Association, the worldwide installed capacity of commissioned hydropower plants rose by 21,900 MW in 2017. This was a record increase in one year.[7]

Hydropower is a good fit with solar and wind power. The generation of hydropower can be ramped up or down in a couple of minutes. As both solar and wind power are intermittent, hydropower will greatly help in stabilizing electric grids.

FOSSIL FUELS: These comprise mainly coal, oil and gas. They have been deposited over the hundreds of millions of years by living organisms, which thrived on sunlight, either directly or indirectly. These are not renewable sources of energy and are finite in their supply. As oil and gas fields and coal mines get depleted, newer ones have to be discovered, which are often more difficult and expensive to access. That is one reason for the continuous rise in the prices of fossil fuels.

Moreover, the living organisms, which laid down these deposits, sequestered huge amounts of carbon from the carbon dioxide in the air and increased the oxygen content of the air, which made animal life, including us, possible in the first place. By burning fossil fuels, we are reversing that process with not yet fully understood consequences. At the start of the Industrial Revolution some 250 years ago, carbon dioxide levels in the air were about 280 ppm (parts per million). The levels have now crossed 400 ppm and are rising. To put this in perspective, the planet has not seen these levels for possibly 25 million years, since the early Oligocene, when the earth was a very different place with a totally dissimilar climate than what we have today.[8] We are already witnessing global warming and a rise in extreme weather patterns.

We know that we should limit the rise of greenhouse gases, or in other words, limit the use of fossil fuels. The Paris Climate Agreement negotiated in 2015 by 196 countries aims to do just that.

However, agreement or no agreement, because of technological breakthroughs in the area of renewable energy, fossil fuels are becoming increasingly uncompetitive. In 1960, fossil fuel energy consumption as a per cent of total consumption was 94 per cent. By 2015, when the Paris agreement was negotiated, it was already 79.68 per cent.[9] A glance at the LCOE table will tell us why. Coal is the most expensive fossil fuel. It is not surprising that coal power is reducing.

No amount of political will is going to reverse this trend. President Trump made revitalizing the coal industry a centrepiece of his 2016 campaign. After coming to power, he did what he could to promote coal. He withdrew America from the Paris climate change agreement and rolled back the Clean Power Plan, but it came to nothing. No new coal-fired plants have been built in the US since 2016. Thirty-six coal-fired plants have been retired since he came to power and thirty more have announced they will close.[10] Economic compulsions prevail over political will.

By the same set of facts, Greta Thunberg, the teenage Swedish climate activist who is campaigning against fossil fuels, will succeed. It is not her iconic efforts that will make her succeed as much the fact that she is on the right side of history.

There is a lesson here for all politicians who attempt to block technologically ushered changes in order to protect jobs. They will find themselves to be on the wrong side of history. When the benefits to be reaped from the changes are huge, nothing will thwart those changes.

The rapid proliferation of solar and wind power has little to do with Green activists. It was preordained by technology and economics. The Greens just happened to be there at the right time making the right noise. The same is true of the Paris Climate Agreement. The shift to renewables would have happened with or without them.

Apart from releasing carbon dioxide into the atmosphere, fossil fuels cost money. All renewable sources of energy are free. Sunlight, wind and water rushing downhill do not cost anything. Fossil fuels have extraction costs and since they are not evenly distributed across the globe, places which have fossil fuel deposits tend to extract the maximum price that markets can bear.

Fossil fuels do, however, have an advantage over most renewable sources. They are flexible. If you need more energy or less energy at any particular time, you simply burn more fuel or less. Unlike solar or wind energy, you are not dependent on sunny days or windy ones. Fossil fuels first extracted their energy from sunlight over millions of years. One way of looking at fossil fuels is to regard them as energy storage batteries, which have stored solar energy over long periods of time. We must then consider the breakthroughs in current energy storage batteries if we are to completely do away with fossil fuels.

BIOFUELS: Biofuels are fuels derived from contemporary biomass, rather than ancient fossilized fuels like coal or oil. Biofuels are considered to be carbon neutral, because while they release carbon dioxide when burnt, that carbon has just recently been sequestered. Biofuels may be carbon neutral, but like all carbon-based fuels they too, release particulate matter into the atmosphere, and in that regard, are not as clean as other renewable energies.

The raw stock for biofuels can come either from crops specially planted for that purpose, such as corn, soya, jatropha and others. There is also some early promise from growing algae to be converted to biofuel. It can also come from the waste material from agricultural sources, such as husk from rice milling and bagasse from sugar cane crushing.[11] While a case can be made out for the production of biofuels from biological waste, it makes no sense to produce biofuels from specially planted energy crops. The reason for that is the wastage of three valuable resources, namely, sunlight, water and land.

The efficiency of a plant in converting sunlight to energy is typically between 1 per cent and 2 per cent. Some of this energy is used by the plant itself, for its metabolism needs, leaving less than half a per cent harvestable energy in the form of corn kernels or potato starch or other plant produce.[12] Water is also needed to grow these crops. Currently, photovoltaic solar panels routinely harvest 20 per cent of the sunlight that falls on them and are likely to soon increase this to over 20 per cent. Also, solar panels do not need water. Even at current efficiencies, it takes fifty times as much land for plants to tap the sun's energy as it does for solar cells. Growing crops for energy is at a dead end.

NUCLEAR ENERGY: The heavy elements such as uranium and thorium were formed in a rare cosmic event with the collision of two neutron stars long before the formation of our solar system.[13] Some of the debris of the collision, including the heavy elements, was included in the matter that formed our solar system, including the earth. The energy released by nuclear fission is inherent in these heavy elements and can be tapped by nuclear fission power plants (or atom bombs).

We have learned to harness that energy only about seventy-five years ago. When we first generated nuclear power, expectations from it were high. In 1954, Lewis Strauss, then chairman of the U.S. Atomic Energy Commission, predicted that nuclear power would be 'too cheap to meter.'[14] It has not quite worked out that way.

The LCOE cost of nuclear power is second only to coal. Nuclear power plants are the most expensive to set up on a cost per unit of installed capacity basis. The cost of nuclear fuel is cheaper than fossil fuels but much more expensive when compared with hydroelectric, geothermal, wind or solar, all of which are free. Nuclear power plants are also the most expensive to operate because they require a very highly skilled workforce and also because of multiple safety protocols.[15, 16]

There are two other concerns regarding nuclear power. One is the safety concern in public perception, especially after the Fukushima accident in 2011. The second is the eventual cost of decommissioning the plant. These costs run into hundreds of millions of US dollars and can even exceed a billion dollars. It is a task that takes a couple of decades to complete.[17]

There is, however, a new development in nuclear energy technology, which may dwarf the initial promise of nuclear power. This involves spent fuel, which is both the residue left over from the enrichment of uranium as well as spent fuel rods from nuclear reactors. Spent nuclear fuel is a liability. It is radioactive and must be kept away from people. It is also liable to be misused and must, therefore, be guarded. The storage of spent fuel costs money. If this spent fuel can be used to generate electricity, the cost of the fuel must be regarded to be cheaper than free. That is the new emerging nuclear technology. It can also use naturally occurring uranium fuel without further enrichment.

The most prominent company in this field is TerraPower.[18] The type of reactor they are working on is a class of nuclear fast reactor called travelling wave reactor (TWR). The TWR that TerraPower is designing will be safe without any danger of core meltdown or any radioactive contamination. It would be loaded with mainly non-fissile isotopes of Uranium-238 with enough fuel for an estimated sixty to hundred years. It would then be buried underground where it would unobtrusively keep pouring out electricity.

TerraPower notes that the US alone has 700,000 metric tons of depleted uranium and that 8 metric tons could power 2.5 million homes for a year. Figures for the stocks of depleted uranium worldwide are difficult to come by. If we assume that the US has a third of worldwide stocks, it would mean that the world has about 2.1 million tons of depleted uranium. The world's population is about 7,500 million people. Again assuming five people to a household (some countries have large families), it means there are 1,500 million households worldwide. Calculating at 8 tons for 2.5 million households, it shows that there is currently enough depleted uranium in the world to power all the world's households for 437 years at US energy consumption levels. At the far more modest average worldwide consumption levels, the period would be closer to a thousand years from an existing source of energy. It sounds almost like a fairytale. Can it possibly become reality?

The list of people backing this project is impressive. TerraPower is partly funded by the US Department of Energy and Los Almos National Laboratory. A primary investor is Bill Gates who is also the chairman of the company since its inception in 2010. In December 2011, India's Reliance Industries announced that it had bought a minority stake in TerraPower and its chairman Mukesh Ambani will join the board of the company.[19] Prominent equity investors have also invested in the company. I mention the promoters behind the venture to drive home the point that it may not be a fairytale.

In September 2015, TerraPower signed an agreement with China National Nuclear Corporation to build a prototype 600 MWe (Megawatts electric) reactor in China during 2018 to 2025. Commercial power plants, generating 1150 MWe were planned for the late 2020s.

In October 2018, in accordance with the stance the Trump administration has taken towards China, the US secretary of energy said that the US 'cannot ignore the national security implications of China's efforts to obtain nuclear technology outside of established processes of US–China civil nuclear cooperation.' New licences and extension of old licences for US companies wishing to work with the Chinese government were stopped.

This is a setback for TerraPower and will delay the project a few years. This is unfortunate because nuclear energy is the only carbon-free scalable source of energy that is available twenty-four hours a day. At a lecture in Peking University, Gates said TWR as nuclear energy was 'dramatically safer and substantially cheaper.'

However, with the advantages the technology has over other sources of energy, TWR reactors will surely get built. We have to wait for a few more years and one day, Lewis Srauss's 1954 prediction about electricity being too cheap to meter may yet come true.

WIND ENERGY: Windmills first appeared in Persia in the ninth century and then later across the rest of Asia and Europe. These mills were mostly used for either grinding grain or pumping water. Wind turbines are windmills that use wind to generate electricity. The first wind turbines were built by the end of the nineteenth century. These were relatively small and were all below 100 kW each. In 1941, the first wind turbine of over 1 MW, known as the Smith-Putnam turbine, was built in Vermont, USA.[20]

For the next sixty-odd years, the installation of wind power capacity grew, but slowly. Thereafter, it took off. The worldwide installed capacity in 2006 was 74.15 Gigawatts (GW) and by 2018, it was 591.5 GW with a growth rate averaging more than 12 per cent over the past four years.[21] Greenpeace and the Global Wind Energy Council have released a two-yearly status report, which estimates that wind energy could be supplying 19 per cent of the world's electricity by 2030 and 25 to 30 per cent by 2050.[22] Denmark is already generating 38 per cent of its electricity through wind power.

While wind power is clean, non-polluting and climate-friendly, the impetus for the rapid roll-out of wind power lies in economics. The price of wind energy is already as low as two to six US cents per kilowatt-hour, depending on the location. The price of electricity from fossil fuels ranges between five and seven US cents per kilowatt-hour.[23]

There are a few new developments taking place that are likely to make wind power yet more attractive and cheaper still.

Because of various design and material improvements, the capacity of wind turbines is increasing. Capacity factor is the efficiency of the turbine. It is the power generated as a percentage of the designed capacity. From 2004 to 2011, it was 32.1 per cent. Recently, the floating offshore turbines in the Hywind Scotland project hit 65 per cent of capacity. That is more than doubling the efficiency in just eight years from 2011.[24]

The generator in a wind turbine is what converts the motion of the blades into electricity. Consisting of copper coils and rotating magnets, it is a very heavy part of the wind turbine and limits the size and therefore, the capacity of the windmill. A consortium of five European countries—Denmark (coordinator), Germany, France, UK and the Netherlands undertook a project to build a superconductive generator. The project was named ECOSWING. The generator was 40 per cent lighter than conventional generators, considerably cheaper and, at super-cold temperatures with almost no resistance, it enabled energy flows, 100 times greater than standard generators. It was run successfully for seven months until April 2019.[25] This technology is not yet in commercial use, but I imagine it soon will be, increasing efficiency and paving the way for larger wind turbines.

Larger is important. Essentially, the ability of any windmill to capture the energy of wind depends on the area swept by the blades as the wind turns them. It is not a linear relationship. The area of a circle is a function of the square of the radius or in the case of windmills, the square of the length of the blades. If the length of the blades is doubled, their ability to capture energy goes up by four times. If it is tripled, that ability increases nine times. Also, wind speeds increase with altitude. Thus, the taller the turbine, the faster it spins and the more energy it can generate.

Apart from its engineering aspects, one major constraint in making really large blades is the problem of transporting the blades from the manufacturing facility to the site of the wind turbine. It is quite literally a roadblock.

To circumvent this roadblock, work has started on additive manufacturing (3D printing) of large blades at the site of the turbines. The US department of energy set up a consortium of two main national laboratories, Sandia National Laboratories and the Oak Ridge National Laboratory as well as TPI Composites, the nation's largest independent manufacturer of wind turbines, to do just that. They successfully designed and printed the moulds for a 13-metre blade in 2018.[26] The 3D printing of blades the length of a football field is not far away.[27] The current process of making wind turbines is very expensive and highly labour-intensive. It is also not easy to make the blades with more complex geometry. The new 3D printed blades will be as complex as desired, much faster to make and not be labour-intensive. They will be cheaper.

Eric Loth, an engineering professor at the University of Virginia, has a goal to build a tower that is 500 metres high and to use 3D printed blades with more complex geometry, which would allow the turbine to generate up to 50 MW of electricity.[28]

With these two new developments of lighter, more efficient generators and large 3D printed blades having been successfully tried out just recently, we will soon see larger and more efficient wind turbines. The projection of 19 per cent of the world's electricity being produced by 2030 may well be exceeded. Even without these two developments being implemented, GE is building its gigantic, state-of-the-art wind turbine called the Haliade-X. The structure will reach 260 metres above sea level with 107-metre blades and can generate 12–14 MW with an energy factor of 63 per cent.[29,30] When the two new developments are in place, Professor Loth's plan will likely materialize. Keep in mind that, with a total structure height of 500 metres, the hub of the wind turbine would be a little more than 250 metres tall. There are hundreds of buildings in the world that are over 250 metres tall. The idea of a simple strong structure 250 metres high that could deliver free energy of 50 MW would be irresistible. In the not-too-distant future, there could be thousands of Professor Loth's structures dotting the globe.

SOLAR PHOTOVOLTAIC (PV) ENERGY: Solar PV is the direct conversion of sunlight into electricity. The first thing we have to grasp about solar energy is that it is incredibly abundant. The earth receives 430 quintillion Joules of energy from the sun each hour. In comparison, the total amount of energy that all humans use in a full year is 410 quintillion Joules. In other words, the earth receives more energy in an hour than humans use in a year.[31] When we talk about the efficiency of solar panels, it is not about parsimoniously using a scarce resource. It is about the cost of electricity generated and the area needed to do so. Unlike sunlight, both money and suitable space for putting up solar panels are in limited supply. The greater the efficiency of a solar panel, the lesser will be the requirements of both money and space to generate a unit of electricity.

The price of solar power depends on two factors. One is the capital cost of putting up the solar panels to generate 1 Watt of electricity and the other is the efficiency of the panels. The lower the capital cost and the higher the efficiency, the lower will be the cost of solar power.

Below is a short Table giving the capital cost of installing one Watt of solar photovoltaic (PV) capacity. It shows how capital costs for solar PV installations have dropped between 2010 and 2018 for different types of PV installations. The prices are American prices in US dollars.[32]

Type of Installation	*2010*	*2018*
Residential (6.2 kW)	7.34	2.79
Commercial (200 kW)	5.43	1.83
Utility scale (100MW) Fixed Tilt	4.63	1.06
Utility scale (100MW) One Axis Tracker	5.52	1.13

In the case of utility scale solar power, over a period of eight years, capital costs have dropped to a fifth of what they were. The cost of all solar installations is set to drop further.

The efficiency of solar cells is increasing. In 1954, Bell Laboratories made the first solar cells with an efficiency of 1 per cent. In 1955, Hoffman Electronics introduced photovoltaic products with an efficiency of 2 per cent and an energy cost of USD 1,785 per Watt.[33] The efficiency of commercial solar panels being made today is about 20 per cent and capital costs are down to USD 1.13 per Watt. The price of solar power has consequently plummeted.

It is dropping faster than we are able to predict. In 2010, the EIA predicted an average price of solar electricity to be 4.88 cents per kWh in 2019 in constant dollars.[34] As we can see from the Los Angeles PPA, it is less than half that price in inflated dollars. I do not know of any prediction that has fully anticipated the rapid drop of solar PV prices.

Can we expect these low prices to fall further? The answer is yes. There are more than ten different laboratory tests of multijunction cells that have achieved efficiencies of over 40 per cent. The national Renewable Energy Laboratory (NREL) has achieved 47.1 per cent efficiency.[35] While the efficiency achieved in laboratories may never be duplicated commercially, with thousands of researchers working all over the world to improve the performance of solar cells, the efficiency of commercial solar cells is likely to cross 30 per cent in the near future.

Almost all solar cells are made of silicon. A new class of materials has emerged, with none of the drawbacks of silicon. It is cheap, easy to work with and promises efficiencies greater than silicon. The material is perovskite.

Perovskite is a calcium titanium oxide mineral. Its name is also applied to a class of minerals having the same crystal structure. Perovskites are plentiful and cheap and can be tweaked chemically for different purposes, including making solar cells. Perovskite solar cells were first made in 2009 with an efficiency of 3.8 per cent. In June 2018, Oxford Photovoltaics achieved a conversion rate of 27.3 per cent. This exceeds the 26.7 efficiency world record for a single-junction silicon solar cell.[36]

Unlike silicon solar cells, perovskite cells can be manufactured with simpler wet chemistry and solvent techniques, such as blade coating, spray coating, inkjet printing, screen printing, all of which have the potential to be scaled up. Traditional solar cells require expensive, multistep processes, conducted at high temperatures of about 1000° C, in a high vacuum in special clean room facilities. Perovskite cells can be printed on many substrates, including glass or film.[37] They are semi-transparent and can cover every sun-facing window in every building or indeed every building itself. They could be on cars, including windows or on any sun-exposed surface we can imagine.

There are estimates that the capital cost of perovskite solar panels could be just ten to twenty US cents per Watt as against USD 1.13, being the lowest cost so far for silicon solar cells. NREL is making progress towards scalable roll-to-roll fabrication of perovskite solar cells. To get an idea of what this could mean, in 2005, the Mitsubishi Diamond Star was the world's largest printing press with a printing speed of 90,000 full colour ninty-six-page broadsheet copies per hour. This is nearly one million square metres per hour. The world added 104 GW of solar power in 2018. Solar power generates about 200 Watts per square metre.[38] The world added about 500 billion square metres of solar cells in 2018. Just one hundred printing presses like the Mitsubishi Diamond Star could double the entire world's solar panels installed in 2018. We are headed towards electricity costs of well below one US cent per kWh.

The prognosis is clear. Solar PV and wind power will capture increasing portions of the energy pie, progressively reducing the share of coal, nuclear, oil and gas. However, both solar and wind have a drawback. Both are intermittent. No solar power can be generated at night or when the sky is overcast. Wind power is only generated when the wind blows. There is a need for batteries to store power for when it is not being generated.

Our capacity to tap renewable sources of energy is well on the way to meeting all our needs. Work on batteries to provide for periods when renewable power is not available as also for powering cars, trucks and perhaps also airplanes is ongoing. German ministers are not known for making exaggerated statements and when Anja Karliczek, German minister of education and research says, 'battery technology is an existential matter,'[39] it underlines the urgency with which research on both improving the performance and lowering the cost of batteries is going on the world over.

According to Bloomberg New Energy Finance, the average global cost of lithium-ion batteries in 2018 was about USD 175 per kWh down from nearly USD 1,200 in 2010. That is seven times cheaper in eight years. The US department of energy calculates that once battery costs fall below USD 125 per kWh, owning and operating an electric car will be cheaper than a gas (petrol) car in most parts of the world.[40]

Batteries currently may be the most researched and experimented subject in universities and research labs across the world. The race to develop the best electricity storage systems is frenetic. The details being released about the research are sparse. The researchers are aware that there is a large pot of gold at the end of this particular rainbow and they are careful of releasing details that may help rivals. The research that is going on is not just about improving the performance of lithium-ion batteries but many other materials that can be used for electricity storage. Tantalizing tidbits of information keep leaking out of research centres periodically about major breakthroughs in the performance of new batteries.

Many companies are in the process of commercialization of sodium-ion batteries. John Goodenough, the person who designed the lithium-ion battery and was awarded the Nobel Prize in Chemistry in 2019 is now a professor at the University of Texas, Austin. He hints at some sort of a vitrified sodium-ion battery, which will have twice the energy density of lithium-ion batteries and be chargeable in minutes instead of hours. Novasis Energies Inc., which originated from Professor Goodenough's group, has developed a sodium-ion battery close in performance to lithium-ion batteries. Faradion Limited, founded in 2011 in the UK, is another such company, which has achieved energy density similar to lithium-ion batteries. There are many other such ventures that are at different levels of success. Once sodium-ion batteries are brought into use, battery prices will drop significantly as sodium is many times cheaper than lithium and as abundant as the oceans.

Work on lithium-ion batteries has not stopped. Switzerland's Innolith claims to have made the world's first 1,000 Watt hour per kilogram rechargeable battery. This is four times Tesla's best of 250. A battery with that density would be able to power an electric car for 620 miles or 1000 kilometres on a single charge.[41]

Aluminum as a battery is a new development and it appears to be very promising. The process of manufacturing aluminum is simple to narrate. The ore containing aluminum is called bauxite and is abundant on the earth. Bauxite is processed chemically to obtain alumina, which is aluminum oxide. Alumina is converted into aluminum by an electrolytic process using large amounts of energy. When using aluminum as a source of energy in the presence of water that acts as a catalyst, the energy used to make the aluminum from alumina is released and can be tapped. The aluminum reverts back to alumina, which can be converted back to aluminum using renewable wind or solar energy, effectively making aluminum into a high-density energy storage battery. Alchemy Research, an Israeli company, managed to power electric vehicles using energy stored in aluminum grain. Aluminum is a very dense energy store. It can accommodate twice the amount of energy as gasoline in the same volume. It can also store eighty times more energy per kilogram than today's best lithium-ion battery. The outcome of this method, says company CEO Gideon Yampolsky, 'is essentially an electric vehicle that is able to reach 2,400 kilometres on a fuel tank that is the size of a standard fuel tank. A regular car that works on fuel is able to reach only 700–800 kilometres.'[42] An Indian start-up, Log 9 Materials, has demonstrated a car run on their aluminum battery capable of going 1000 kilometres.[43] With the energy density demonstrated by aluminum as a battery, it is possible that aluminum may one day be driving ships and airplanes as well.

In another approach to energy storage, green hydrogen has started to be used. Green hydrogen is hydrogen that is produced by electrolysis of water. This method is completely non-polluting. The only inputs are electricity and water and the only outputs are hydrogen and oxygen. When the hydrogen is burnt as a source of power, the only emission is water. The earlier way of producing hydrogen in commercial quantities by exposing fossil fuels to steam is not even remotely zero-carbon and is known as grey hydrogen. Companies are working to develop electrolysers that can produce green hydrogen as cheaply as grey hydrogen. Meanwhile energy companies are starting to integrate electrolysers directly into renewable power projects. A consortium of companies behind a project called Gigastack, plan to equip a offshore wind farm with 100 MW of electrolysers to generate green hydrogen at an industrial scale. This technology is being invested in by many countries. Australia wants to export hydrogen that it would produce using its plentiful solar and wind power. China aims to put one million hydrogen fuel-cell vehicles on the road by 2030.[44]

The new story of energy will then be in place. It will be clean renewable energy, mainly from solar, wind and hydroelectric sources with added inputs from the travelling wave depleted uranium reactors if and when that becomes a reality. The age of fossil fuels will be over. Energy will be far cheaper than it is today.

The very texture of the production and use of energy will change. Traditional power plants, whether nuclear, thermal or hydroelectric, needed vast outlays of money and time. The generating capacity of these plants was measured in hundreds of MWs. Economic development, travels along wires carrying electricity, as they radiate out from the generating plant. No wires means no development. It is a completely different story with wind and especially solar power. It is independent of cross-country wiring. It is about installing as much power generation as needed anywhere at all. With solar power, it can be installed a few kilowatts at a time and with wind energy, at a few hundred kilowatts at a go. It is entirely conceivable that Professor Loth's wind energy towers could be covered with perovskite solar cell sheets and could be generating some solar energy too and storing energy in battery banks within the structure and simply be known as energy towers.

As far as access to energy is concerned, we have been liberated from the tyranny of the developments and geographical circumstances. Energy can now be accessed anywhere on earth, without having to consider where existing power plants and power lines are located. The effects of this will be profound, especially in the less developed parts of the globe. The word 'remote' will vanish from the energy lexicon. It is perhaps too early for us to fully imagine the changes that will be wrought.

It is only a matter of time that the infrastructure for the entire cycle of renewable energy, from generation to storage to end use will be complete and put up as quickly as possible. It will, however, take a few more years for the roll-out of renewables to ramp up to the level where existing conventional energy sources, such as coal, nuclear, oil and gas plants can be dismantled. Until then, it would be prudent to resist the call from Green activists, especially in Europe and America, who wish to quickly dismantle existing facilities, or else a country could face unpleasant surprises, such as grid collapses. Once we have sufficient renewables capacity, we will see the automatic demise of fossil fuel and traditional nuclear plants. With solar and wind prices declining to less than the one US cent per kWh range, fossil fuels and nuclear plants will simply not be able to compete. Any new nuclear plants that are then put up will be purely for strategic purposes.

In this chapter we have seen the developments taking place in all parts of the energy cycle. Let us now try and imagine what these coming changes will result in and how all our lives will be affected. That is the essence of this chapter. This is an exercise I shall do at the end of every remaining chapter in the first part of the book. I have not done this exercise for the previous chapter on Artificial Intelligence, as AI is an enabling technology, which does not much impact us directly. When coupled with almost any other human activity, it has the potential to dramatically change our lives.

Understanding the changes coming our way will form the bedrock of the second part of this book, which is about strategies on how to cope with the coming changes.

The consequences of the coming changes have been divided into two groups from the standpoint of the average man or woman.

Desirable Consequences:

1. Electricity will become very cheap.
2. The generation of electricity will become more dispersed. Local area grids will become the norm and be able to supply electricity cheaper than national grids. Houses with the ability to put up enough solar panels will not only be able to generate enough electricity for household needs but also enough to charge their electric vehicles and perhaps supply some electricity to the grid.
3. Goods will become cheaper. All industrial processes that use electricity will be cheaper to run, giving a downward impetus to prices.
4. With the reduction and eventual near elimination of fossil fuels, the air around us will become cleaner and it will be a harbinger for better health.
5. Reduced fossil fuel usage will result in reduced carbon dioxide emissions and a lessening impact on global warming.

Worrisome Consequences:

1. Jobs will be lost. We have already started losing jobs in coal mining and in coal-fired power plants. The next jobs to reduce

will be the oil and gas field exploration jobs and then the oil and gas field production and refining jobs.

2. Along with the reduced output of fossil fuels, the fossil fuel transportation jobs will reduce. These jobs include shipping jobs as in tankers, gas carriers and bulk carriers for coal, trucking and railroad jobs to wherever fossil fuels have to be moved. These will not be replaced with anything. Electricity moves on wires and not by road or rail or sea.
3. Certainly, new jobs will be created for the manufacture and setting up of solar panels and windmills. The manufacture of these will be largely automated processes, yielding fewer jobs. The setting up of both solar panels and wind turbines will generate jobs, but these are one-time jobs with solar panels and windmills having an operating life of about twenty-five to thirty years. The job losses will be far more than the new jobs created.

3

MANUFACTURING

Most of us are aware that with more complex machines and increased automation, some manufacturing jobs are being lost or are under threat. We are also probably aware that it is a combination of artificial intelligence (AI), machine learning and the Internet of Things (IoT), along with robots that is responsible for the job losses. However, few of us realize the magnitude of the coming changes.

Located ninety minutes west of Tokyo, in the shadows of Mount Fuji, Oshino in Japan is home to 9,000 people, which means, that in any given year, the 60,000 robots produced at the town's FANUC (the name is an acronym of Fuji Automated Numerical Control) plant outnumber humans by roughly seven to one. As for how many humans it takes to construct these 5,000 robots a month, don't bother counting—the robots build themselves, test and inspect themselves. A generation ago, many people, including manufacturing executives themselves, would have considered such a facility as science fiction or centuries away. To be certain, it is one of the world's first 'lights-out factories' where 24×7 operation is a reality and there are no humans who need light to find their way about. Intelligent robots create computerized offsprings that are capable of Machine Learning and computer vision,[1] just like them. Robots can now make more robots, sometimes with the lights out, much as humans can make more humans.

If robots can make robots, they should also be able to make anything that is simpler. Just how complicated are robots to make? There is no simple answer to this question. When we think of industrial robots, we have to abandon any images we may have in our minds of Honda's iconic humanoid robot, ASIMO, or the Star-wars robots, C-3PO or R2-D2. Industrial robots are in no way as versatile as these iconic robots. At the same time, industrial robots are not as locked into a single function as were camshafts.

Camshafts are rotating shafts, which have protuberances or cams, either built into them or attached to them. These cams actuate a series of levers or valves in a particular sequence. Earlier factory automation and the workings of the internal combustion engine depended on camshafts to function. Once built for a particular function, a camshaft could do nothing else. Also, a camshaft had no sensors and continued to do what it was designed to do, regardless of what happened in the production line or inside the engine where it had been installed. If something went wrong on the production line or in the engine, the camshaft could not stop the operation. It just kept rotating until something around it or it itself broke down. The early automated production lines could not be left unattended. Humans had the control. Machines just helped them.

That is not the case today with robotic production lines. These lines are fitted with multiple sensors and algorithms covering all conceivable eventualities. Should an as yet unforeseen event take place, algorithms are updated to include the new incident and if necessary, more sensors added, keeping the facility upgraded continuously. Should the business decide to add another production line, it need not go through the trouble to recruit and train more people. It needs to only duplicate the existing line and double its production in little time. The new production line need not be adjacent to the existing one. It could be anywhere on the planet.

Sceptics who do not see the coming wave of robotic manufacturing can point out with some validity, that the FANUC lights-out plant at Oshino is not necessarily a harbinger of a rapid shift to robotics. FANUC is after all the largest group in the world in the fields of robotics and automation, with a market share of 65 per cent of the global market for the manufacture of computerized numerical control devices. What FANUC has done may not be so easy for other companies, especially smaller ones, to do. That may be so, but they would be missing an important point. If the FANUC plant is manufacturing 5,000 robots a month, it is surely selling 5,000 robots a month, and is selling them to other companies.

Companies that are not robot-making companies are robotizing their manufacturing facilities. In a Philips plant producing electric razors in the Netherlands, robots outnumber the production workers fourteen to one. Camera-maker Canon began phasing out human labour at several of its factories in 2013.[2]

FANUC's clients include numerous US and Japanese automobile and electronics manufacturers. Use of industrial robots has allowed companies like Panasonic in Amagasaki, Japan to run factories which produce 2 million TV sets a month (mostly high-end plasma LCD screens) with just twenty-five people.[3]

I do not know the salaries of the twenty-five people working at Panasonic's TV factory. However, let us assume that the average pay packet of the twenty-five people is half a million US dollars a year. That means that the labour cost of making 24 million high-end TVs is USD 12.5 million. That is just about fifty US cents per high-end TV. With few manufacturing jobs available, the bargaining position of labour is going to erode. Labour's share of the profits of every manufacturing business will decrease while inequality will increase.

For those who may think that automation in production facilities in India is only a distant possibility, it will be interesting to note that FANUC, the company whose robots make more robots without human intervention, has a subsidiary in India, FANUC India, since 1992. It is headquartered in Bengaluru. According to their website, they have offices in twenty-one locations across the country. Automation in Indian factories is happening now.

The time for cheap labour as an advantage is fast running out. Fewer companies are going to be setting up manufacturing plants in distant lands where labour is cheaper. China's status as the 'factory to the world' is going to erode. India's recent thrust of 'Make in India' is perhaps thirty years too late in the coming. The factories of the world will be located where the markets of the world are. India, being a large market, will benefit from the development of automated factories for making almost everything. Currently, India imports far more manufactured goods than it exports. It will become easier for India to manufacture the goods it now imports. India, being a large market, will cause manufacturing plants to come up within India to cater to its needs. It will be a different story for China. China today has the most sophisticated infrastructure to manufacture all manner of goods. Low wages gave China the initial advantage to start manufacturing for the world. The gradual installation of manufacturing infrastructure added to this advantage. With the increasing installation of automated factories, China's lower costing labour will no longer be an advantage. The demand for goods made in China and shipped to other places will diminish and cause loss of jobs in China. Local area manufacture of goods in automated plants will reverse globalization. China, being perhaps the largest beneficiary of globalization, will lose the most. India will be able to locally manufacture much of its growing requirements within the country and will benefit accordingly.

Deglobalization will benefit India. India has a population of 1.3 billion. That was the global population in 1860. We do not need to export as desperately as many smaller countries need to. The size of our own market is large enough to sustain a sizable production base in every segment of the economy.

The window of opportunity, during which developing countries could export their way to relative prosperity as well as provide employment to their burgeoning millions in manufacturing, is fast closing.

So far, the examples I have given of robotic factories are all of extremely large companies like Philips, Panasonic and Canon. Soon however, robotics is going to reach medium and small enterprises. An index of average robot prices and labour compensation, for the years 1990 to 2015, with sources from the Economist Intelligence Unit, IMB, International Robot Federation, US Social Security data and McKinsey analysis, is illustrative of the trend. It pegs the index at 100 for both robot prices and labour compensation in 1990. By 2015, comparative labour costs had climbed to 210, whereas the robot costs had dwindled to fifty.

Largely because of Moore's law, robot prices will continue to drop. Soon smaller companies will be able to afford robotic manufacturing facilities. It will not be a matter of choice for them. The first companies in any industry that shift to robotics, will have better product quality, lower costs and enhanced capacities. They will drive the companies that do not robotize out of business.

Companies like FANUC and other robot companies will need to have fewer people in manufacturing robots than in selling them. The sales teams will not only need to sell robots but also guide the integration of robots into existing production lines. This will open up a whole new line of employment as facilitators or integrators. Before we start viewing this as a large job opportunity opening up, we need to keep in mind that every sale that a facilitator makes, will result in the loss of at least a few existing jobs. Facilitators are likely to be seen as job-destroying agents or a swarm of locusts that come and denude the landscape of jobs.

Robotic manufacturing is not only about cost saving. There are many processes that can only be done by varying degrees of automation. The accuracy that robots can achieve is measured in microns. A micron is a millionth of a metre. Human hands cannot deliver such accuracy. Any goods made by robots are almost by definition more precise than those made by other methods. A robotically produced item is likely to be a superior product. It will be difficult for traditionally produced goods to compete on quality parameters. Goods such as the SIM card in your phone or the solar cells producing electricity cannot be produced by human labour alone. A degree of automation is always involved in the manufacture of such items.

I recently viewed on YouTube an eight-minute clip, put out by Meyer Burger Technology AG, a Swiss company with worldwide operations in engineering and photovoltaic systems. The clip showed the manufacture of solar cells with hetero-junction technology. In the clip, there are rows and rows of impressive-looking machines making the solar cells. The only humans to be seen were those with trolleys, shifting trays of solar cells in various stages of manufacture, from one row to another. It is very likely that when Meyer Burger makes their next facility, they will eliminate humans entirely and enter the growing list of 'lights-out' manufacturing facilities, with no humans on the shop floor.

Robotic factories will also have the ability to carry out industrial processes in extreme conditions, such as extreme heat or cold, or in high pressures and in a vacuum, or in any ambience that is inimical to human existence. That could also include radiation or the presence of gases that are not conducive to life. This ability could pave the way for new processes and products, which are not possible with human workers.

On a somewhat futuristic note, Caterpillar, the manufacturer of heavy-duty earthmoving and mining equipment, is working with NASA to develop robotic equipment to mine the moon for water and materials to build a permanent lunar base, once NASA returns to the moon in 2024.[4] Caterpillar has been developing autonomous mining equipment for mining here on the earth and was perhaps the logical partner to tie up with NASA for lunar mining. The extreme temperature, the cosmic radiation and the vacuum, which exists on the lunar surface, does not bother robotic miners.

In the not-too-distant future, when robotic manufacture has become the norm and every factory is delivering near perfect products, how will one manufacturer compete against another? What will differentiate them? There will be a paradigm shift in the basics of doing business. Innovation will still matter, in fact, increasingly so. The other parameters will change. Labour skills will matter diminishingly. The arena of competition will change from the efficiency of factories to the efficiency of societies as a whole. The ease of doing business in different countries will become the differentiator. Infrastructure and the robustness of supply chains will matter. The sanctity of contracts and a responsive legal system will be crucial. Justice delivery systems will shift to the front line of the efficiency wars. It will no longer be sufficient for the wheels of justice to grind exceedingly fine. They must turn quickly too. The countries that do a better job of having the physical and social infrastructure in place, will attract more manufacturing facilities and corner more of the limited number of manufacturing jobs that will exist.

Let us look at the consequences of the coming changes in manufacturing practices.

Desirable Consequences:

1. The quality of manufactured goods will improve.
2. Manufactured goods will become cheaper.
3. Because of the precision of robotic manufacture, wastage of raw materials will reduce, putting a lesser load on the environment.
4. With the enhanced capabilities of robotic manufacture, new products will surely be made possible and be produced. It is difficult at this time to foretell what these new products could be.
5. Jobs to sell robotic factories and integrate robots into existing factories will be created.

Worrisome Consequences:

1. Jobs will be lost in the manufacturing sector.
2. The jobs lost to robots will far outnumber the jobs created for selling robotic manufacturing processes.
3. Inequality will increase.

4

THE SHARING ECONOMY

I started writing this book seeing and reading about the technological changes taking place in almost all areas of our lives. I felt that such major developments would not merely increase the efficiency of some processes but would impact the very fabric of our societies. The plan was to enumerate all the breakthroughs and developments taking place around us in the first part of the book and devote the second part of the book looking at what we might do to take advantage of all the coming changes and fashion a world to our liking.

However, new developments do not always fit into preslotted spaces. For this book, the sharing economy was one such development. The sharing economy arises when we start sharing things, often for a small price, instead of buying new things. The sharing economy was enabled with the development of communication platforms created for the purpose. Like other new developments, the sharing economy too, induced changes in our lives and also our economies. If more goods are shared, less will be bought. In that sense, the sharing economy is part of the problem as it reduces the demand and therefore, the manufacture of goods and reduces jobs. On the other hand, sharing platforms also enable the creation and sharing of jobs, albeit of a temporary nature. This part of the sharing economy is often referred to as the Gig economy. In that sense, it is part of the solution. I spent a couple of days trying to figure out where to put this chapter and leave it to the reader to decide if this is the proper place to put this chapter in. Let us now look a little closer at the sharing economy.

On an individual level, it makes good economic sense to share an asset, which is lying idle and get some money in return for lending it. For the other party too, it makes equally good sense to, let us say, borrow a power tool for a few hours and pay a little money, rather than buying it and then having it lie idle for most of the time. On a macro or societal level too, sharing makes economic sense. If the power tool had not been borrowed but bought instead, the community would have had two power tools, which would both be lying idle for most of the time. Because the second power tool was not bought, the money saved can be used to buy a bicycle or go to the theatre. If the person who buys the bicycle does not use it every day or all the time, the bicycle too can become a part of the sharing economy. A sharing economy encourages the acquisition of more assets by a community, raising the standard of living of the whole community. This is the essence of a sharing economy.

There are, however, detractors, who do not think that the sharing economy is a good idea. Their reasoning is that the sharing of goods depresses the sale and therefore, the manufacture of goods. It depresses jobs. Governments, especially those that levy a high rate of sales tax, are also not enthused by people sharing goods instead of buying them.

If a power tool or bicycle or any other item, costing USD 100, is shared with twenty people during its lifetime and a sharing cost of five US dollars is charged for it, the cost of the item for the original buyer is free, other than the maintenance cost of the good. The sale of twenty such goods has been precluded. If the sales tax is 12 per cent (which is the Goods and Services Tax in India, for most goods and services), the government loses tax revenue, of USD 240. Even if the government manages to capture each of the twenty sharing transactions and taxes them at the same rate of 12 per cent, its tax revenue will be only twelve US dollars. It is easy to see where disenchantment with the sharing economy comes from. Factories would make twenty less power tools or bicycles. Shopkeepers would sell twenty less of these items and the government would lose a minimum of USD 228 in tax revenue.

The community, on the other hand, has saved USD 2,240, which it would have otherwise spent on the cost of the goods and the sales taxes. It would still have access to the goods when needed. Once the realization that having access to an item is as good as having ownership of it sets in, it is a win-win deal for the community. If the power tool is a drill, what you need is the hole it has made and not the tool itself. The money it has saved will permit the community as a whole to buy other goods such as rollerblades or a scuba diving set or whatever else it feels it wants. These new goods could again become a part of the sharing economy, raising the standard of living of the entire community.

But what of the business lost by the factories and shopkeepers and the revenue lost by the government? The eighteenth-century French economist Claude-Frédéric Bastiat examined this problem in his parable about the broken window. In this story, a baker's mischievous son throws a stone and breaks the window of the bakery. The townspeople gather to see what is happening. Some think that the boy has done the economy of the town a service, as the boy's father will have to buy a new window glass from the glazier who, in turn, will spend the money he has earned on something else and so on ad infinitum, kick-starting the town's economy. The townspeople come to believe that breaking windows stimulates the economy. However, the baker had been saving money to buy a new coat, which he will now not be able to buy. Had he bought the coat, the tailor would have spent the money earned on something else, much in the same way that the glazier will now do. The basic difference, as Bastiat pointed out, is that had the window not been broken, the community as a whole would have possessed a window and a coat. It now only has a window.[1]

It is the same with the sharing economy. Buying goods, which will be in storage most of the time, is avoided. Unnecessary duplication of goods is avoided. The money freed up from the needless buying can be used to buy or experience something else. The factories making the power tools or bicycles may have lost some business but factories making something else, or service providers, will gain some. Simply by avoiding unnecessary expenditure on goods that can be shared, the sharing economy enriches a community by giving it access to a greater variety of goods and services.

For a sharing economy to function and thrive, bestowing its munificence on a community, there are only four requirements:

1. There must be idle capacity. It could be of underutilized physical goods, underutilized time so that one's expertise in any field could be offered for sharing, or even spare money which could be put to more productive use through crowdfunding platforms.
2. Widespread communication is necessary to enable people with supply to be able to connect with people with demand. The tradition of lending and borrowing, between friends and neighbours, has long been a standard practice the world over. Earlier, it was not called a sharing economy. It was called being neighbourly. The only people who knew you had a power tool or bicycle to spare occasionally were the people who knew you quite well. It was not until the wide usage of the Internet happened that you could let more people know that you had a particular power tool or bicycle or apartment, which you would be happy to hire out. It was in about 2005 that connectivity became almost universal and also available on smartphones. The sharing economy could not have started before that.

   Airbnb, a home- and room-sharing platform, started in 2008 and was valued at USD 31 billion in 2019. It is now present in over 100,000 cities over the world. In

2019, Airbnb said they have had more than 500 million guest arrivals since they started.[2] Uber, the car ride-sharing platform founded in 2009, crossed the milestone of carrying 10 billion passengers in 2018.[3] TaskRabbit, a platform that matches freelance labour with local demand, started in 2008 and currently has tens of thousands of vetted, background-checked 'Taskers' across a wide variety of categories. This last example of sharing time is also known as the gig economy. A gig is normally referred to a temporary employment for musicians and other entertainers. The term, 'gig economy' means temporary employment in any area.

The gig economy is informal in nature, temporary and consensual. It cannot function under other conditions. Labour unions and government labour departments should not try and muscle into the area. Participants in the gig economy should be able to freely report their earnings and contribute to their savings and retirement needs.

3. The third requirement for having a sharing economy is trust. Without trust, a sharing economy cannot function. How do we create trust? Do we automatically trust strangers? What if the person who borrows your power tool or bicycle does not return those items? This matter of trust has opened up a space for aggregating companies, which do a Know Your Customer (KYC) exercise on customers who wish to use your asset. The KYC exercise provides proof of identity and the whereabouts of the borrower as well as a cursory check of the publicly available record of the person. Beyond the KYC exercise is the respect and fear of the law. There is the underlying threat of legal remedy. If the legal remedy is either non-existent or tardy and expensive in coming, it will put a damper on the lending economy. If you lend out a bicycle, which is not returned and the remedy involves

numerous court appearances, over many years and lawyer fees for every appearance and years awaiting the verdict, you would never rent out your cycle again. Without an expeditious justice delivery system, the entire sharing economy, which can enrich communities, comes to a dead end, aborting the promise of material well-being of the country. Judges, lawyers, law ministries and the whole legal community need to confront the reality that they serve not only the blindfolded goddess of justice in all her pristine glory, but they are also cogs in the omnipresent economic engine. They can also be the cause which impoverishes a country.

Full areas of business ventures have had to be abandoned in countries that have not been able to provide this legal security. In India, for example, the entire self-driving cars-for-hire business is non-existent. The worldwide revenue for this business in 2019 is estimated to be about US$ 124 billion.[5] This area of enterprise has bypassed India because of a lack of legal security. Cars for hire that come with drivers, and are more expensive, are easily available. The sharing economy, which also needs a robust and quick justice delivery system to function, may also bypass India and all countries that are unable to evolve such a system.

Car-sharing platforms, such as Uber, are doing well in India. The main reason for that is the cars that are shared are always in full control and possession of the car owner or his salaried employee and do not need to depend upon the legal system to regain possession of their assets. Sharing models that hand over temporary possession of their assets will not do well in India and other countries without a prompt justice delivery system. The enriching sharing economy will bypass such countries.

4. The fourth requirement to kick-start the sharing economy

is the clarity of laws that encourage the sharing of assets. Airbnb is present in India. I recently tried to Google and find out if Airbnb was legal in India. My findings were confusing. While some viewed it as being legal, others did not. Opinions on both sides were strewn with caveats. This ambiguity must go. The crux of a sharing economy is that it encourages the maximum utilization of assets. All countries, especially one that is light on assets, cannot afford to ignore the sharing economy.

The sharing economy is quite new, barely ten to twelve years old. It is thriving and growing rapidly where it can. It is becoming a significant portion of the overall economy. Anything that is new brings with itself its own set of problems and opportunities. A legal framework has to be created to mitigate the problems and enhance the opportunities. The framework has to be focused on the future and not on the past. The car ride-sharing platforms, for example, will have their own issues, which will have to be dealt with, but these issues cannot include the problems of the yellow taxis, which are all but history. No amount of legislation can restore them to their earlier prominence.

A few countries have passed some legislation to take advantage of the new opportunities. In 2012, the USA passed the Jumpstart Our Business Startups, or JOBS Act, to encourage funding of small businesses, by easing many of the securities regulations. It is also known as the CROWDFUND Act and creates a way for companies to use crowdfunding to issue securities, which was not previously permitted.[6]

An omnibus Act, covering the entire sharing economy, needs to be enacted by each country, which wishes to benefit from it. The Act must cover all aspects of sharing, from the sharing of goods to the sharing of time and labour as well as the sharing of money as in crowdfunding. The drift of that law must be to enable all sharing rather than hampering it. The time to enact such laws is now. With the rising scarcity of jobs, the smooth functioning of the gig economy, where people can get to do all sorts of temporary jobs, will become crucial. It is going to be equally important for ideas or ventures that are too small to approach banks, to be able to fund the ventures through crowdfunding and create jobs.

Some countries have realized the potential of the sharing economy sooner than others. The Chinese government designated the sharing economy as a national priority in 2015. The size of China's sharing economy was estimated to have reached USD 438 billion in 2018.[7,8] It is further expected to grow by 30 per cent each year for the next three years.[9]

The consequences arising from the sharing economy are fairly straightforward.

Desirable Consequences:

1. As more goods are shared, the lesser will be the goods that are purchased. This will lead to a drop in the cost of living, thereby enriching the community.
2. As lesser goods are bought, the lesser will be manufactured, putting a downward pressure on material resources and the environment.
3. The gig economy will open up a large avenue of informal jobs.

Worrisome Consequences:

1. As lesser goods are bought, the lesser will be manufactured. This will eliminate some manufacturing jobs, which are mostly in the formal sector of the economy.
2. In effect, there will be shift in jobs from the formal to the

informal sector. This could lead to a relook at many laws, including labour laws and taxation laws. It will bring more focus to retirement plans. A more flexible approach to the voluntary reporting of income will need to be encouraged.

5

TRANSPORT AND CONNECTIVITY

I am thrilled. All my childhood science fiction comics are becoming reality. Self-driving cars, self-flying aircraft and ships without helmsmen or crew are on the verge of being commonplace. Hyperloops and yes, even flying cars have been demonstrated. Reusable spacecraft are already here. Human outposts on the moon and settlements on Mars are being seriously planned. In my boyhood years, some sixty years ago, there were two distinct worlds, the science fiction world and the real world. The boundary between the two has blurred.

Changes are coming in every field of human endeavour. It is as if we have attained some critical mass of innovation. In the area of transport, so many new developments are nearing maturity at about the same time that by the end of the 2020s, the manner in which we, and our goods, reach from place to place, will be quite different from how it is today. We are not going to wake up one fine morning and find a new transportation system in place. We will go there in steps. We have already started taking the first steps and those are not baby steps. The basic technology for the coming change is already in place and been demonstrated. What remains is the final tweaking of the technology and its large-scale roll-out.

Perhaps the one thing that will affect our lives the most is self-driving cars and trucks. How technology will impact trucks is easier to imagine. There will be fewer trucks on the roads. While the same number of trucks will be needed to carry the same amount of cargo, there will be no trucks waiting at diners or 'dhabas' as we call them in India, where drivers need to stop to eat, rest or sleep. Automated trucks will drive non-stop until they reach their destination. The mini roadside economy that caters to the need of the drivers will vanish. The productivity of each truck will improve by anywhere between 25 per cent and 50 per cent, bringing down the cost of carrying cargo and needing that many fewer trucks. The jobs that vanish will not be only those of the drivers but also those of the roadside economy.

It is a little more complicated in the case of cars. Ten years ago, there were only three ways to ride a car. You owned and drove your car or employed a chauffeur to drive it for you. You rented a car and drove it, or you hailed a taxi. With the advent of the sharing economy, taxis are all but extinct. With the advent of self-driving cars, private ownership of cars will make no sense whatsoever. It will at least not make any economic sense. If a car can reach you wherever you are in a few minutes and take you wherever you wish to go, without impinging on your privacy and without you being needed to drive it, you would be unlikely to invest in a car and maintain it and drive it, especially if it is cheaper to not own a car. There is, however, no accounting for human vanities. Many people at the start of the automated cars era may still maintain a car, much as people kept maintaining a horse, long after they stopped using horses as their chief means of transport. To cater to human vanities, companies that hire out these automated cars will probably need to invest in cars of varying luxury levels.

All manner of driving jobs, including those of car-share companies, such as Uber, will vanish. There will be far fewer cars on the road. The manufacture and sale of cars will decrease but by not as much. The fewer cars on the road will, on an average, mean each drive for longer times and distances to cover the same total transport needs as before. The mode of travel will change from human-driven to machine-driven but the need to travel will stay the same if we ignore the reduced travel needed because of better online communication networks. As a consequence of individual cars driving more, they will age and depreciate faster and need to be replaced sooner. After an initial settling down period, car-manufacturing volumes will revert to near current levels. There will be as much pressure on the road space as it is now, but the pressure on parking spaces will drop considerably. A large area of all urban spaces the world over is currently dedicated to the parking of cars. These areas will be freed up for other uses. Automated cars will be mostly electric vehicles and the pollution emanating from the tailpipes of cars will come to an end.

Just how soon can we expect to see automated cars and trucks becoming commonplace? There are very divergent views on this. Steve Wozniak, co-founder of Apple says he does not expect fully automated cars in his lifetime. Technology will need to be able to accommodate 'the dumbest human behind the wheel to take control when an unusual situation comes up.'[1] Elon Musk, the Tesla CEO, thinks differently. In April 2019, he announced his newest plans for disrupting the ride-sharing industry with a fleet of self-driving Teslas that could come as soon as 2020. Mr Musk is given to making grand announcements, which often miss self-imposed deadlines. When he says, 'next year for sure, we will have over one million robotaxis on the road',[2] he may miss this deadline by a year or two, but given the self-driving features of his newest Tesla cars, which can be updated remotely, I think he will get there.

Tesla is not the only company working towards self-driving cars. Every major car manufacturer is working on making automated cars a reality in the near future. General Motors, Ford, Mercedes Benz, Volkswagen, Audi, Nissan, Toyota, BMW and Volvo are all racing to make self-driving cars.[3] Car manufacturers are not the only companies working on this. Technology companies such as Google and Apple have been working on automated cars from about 2009. While Google has been quite open about it, Apple has chosen to be more secretive. It is, however, difficult to hide a project as big as a technology company building self-driving cars. There are several pointers towards this. In 2016, Elon Musk stated that Apple would probably make a compelling electric car, 'It's pretty hard to hide something if you hire over a thousand engineers to do it.'[4] Car ride-sharing companies Uber and Lyft are also pursuing the same goal, often teaming up with software and car manufacturing companies.

Currently, at the end of 2019, self-driven cars have amassed millions of miles test-driving down public roads, honing their algorithms and learning to cope with normal road conditions and traffic. The events that a car can encounter on a road are so varied that they are impossible to foresee and be pre-programmed to handle. Moritz Dechant, group leader for system integration and testing, for Bosch, in Palo Alto, says, 'The complexity of the real world raises the bar for the artificial intelligence we apply. It's very hard to model all potential situations, which your product will later encounter on the street or beside it. A senior citizen in a wheelchair chasing a rabbit: that's just one example of challenging traffic scenarios I'm aware of, recorded by an automated driving prototype. Hence, one big challenge our experts face every day is to improve the vehicle's generic understanding of its surrounding environment and all moving and static objects, as well as the prediction of their behaviour to adapt its own in an optimal way.'[5]

Late in the evening of 18 March 2018, Elaine Herzberg was hit by an Uber automated car and became the first pedestrian fatality of a self-driven car. Her death has been likened to the death of Bridget Driscoll, whose death was the first pedestrian one caused by a motorcar on 17 August 1896. The jury returned a verdict of accidental death. In the case of the automated car accident, it was more of negligence and a casual approach to safety. The car had a built-in emergency braking system, which had been disabled and been replaced by a human safety operator, who was expected to brake when needed. After hours of uneventful automatic driving, I think it is unrealistic to expect a human to constantly stay on knife-edge alertness. The car had detected Elaine Herzberg who was pushing a bicycle across a four-lane road, not at a pedestrian crossing, a full six seconds before the collision. The car had been trying to determine the nature of the object for 4.7 seconds before braking automatically, too late to avoid impact.[6]

Clearly, neither Moritz Dechant of Bosch nor the programmers who had written the algorithms of the Uber car were Indians or had any experience driving on Indian roads. On Indian roads, the unexpected is the norm. It may not be common to see senior citizens on wheelchairs chasing rabbits, but it would not be surprising to find a senior citizen in a wheelchair feeding a cow a snack on a road in the midst of traffic. Jaywalkers are always expected. The nature of the object is only of secondary importance. Of primary importance is the risk of collision. Assessing the risk of collision is not new technology. It has been there since the 1960s, long before the advent of AI. Ships then started being fitted with ARPA, standing for Automatic Radar Plotting Aid, which can calculate the course, speed and expected time to collision with a tracked object.[7] It is gross negligence not to incorporate a similar algorithm in automated cars.

The lessons from that unfortunate accident have been learnt not only by Uber, but also by every entity working on automated cars and will not be readily repeated. That is the promise of AI. Millions of pedestrians have been killed because of human drivers, since the first death of Bridget Driscoll in 1896. The toll on human lives lost to automated cars will not be even a small fraction of that number.

While automated cars may be around the corner and have the most impact on our lives, other transport breakthroughs are equally breathtaking. The flying cars are finally flying. They had long been anticipated. In 1940, Henry Ford famously predicted, 'Mark my words: a combination airplane and motor car is coming. You may smile, but it will come.'[8] A host of major companies around the world are developing flying cars using novel designs.

Designs include multiple rotors as in drones, rotorcraft with folding blades, as well as ducted fan and tilt-rotor vehicles. One of the most exciting designs is from Lilium, in Munich, a Germany-based aviation start-up. Lilium's flying car has thirty-six small, electrically driven jet engines that face downwards on takeoff and then tilt backward for horizontal flight. In October 2019, Lilium demonstrated its flying car capable of carrying five passengers and achieving a speed of 100 kilometres per hour. The company is targeting a speed of 300 kmph as well as a range of 300 kilometres. Lilium plans to launch an air taxi service by 2025. It estimates that a ride from New York's JFK airport to Manhattan will cost seventy dollors and take less than six minutes. It plans to eventually launch a consumer-facing app that lets users hail the jet like they would a Uber taxi.[9] Indeed, no flying car developer is planning on putting a flying car in every garage. All are visualizing some sort of a flying car hiring service.

Among the companies developing flying cars are Uber, Boeing and German start-up Volocopter. Chinese drone manufacturer Ehang has already carried VIPs on its eVTOL in 2018, while Airbus is developing its automated Vahana craft.[10] Uber is not developing flying cars in-house; however, it is catalysing on an ever-expanding industry that seeks to be the answer to the fantasies of urban communities. All developments of flying cars are of Vertical Take Off and Landing (VTOL) design, so that no airstrips or airports are needed for them to operate. Ideally, a flying car should be able to navigate roads and also take to the skies, but hardly any company is trying to do so, mainly because the size of the flying cars is turning out to be somewhat larger than what traffic conditions will permit on most roads. The emerging scenario points towards flying cars landing and taking off from building tops or parking lots, many of which will become redundant because of car sharing. So, while we may not be quite like the Jetsons[11, 12] yet, we will have come very close.

Pilotless aircraft are already a reality. Military drones do not only fly by themselves, take off and land, they also undertake precession bombing missions. The drones have controllers who help in choosing the target to be bombed or photographed but do not fly the planes as such. The controllers seldom are licensed pilots. There is no real reason other than public confidence that pilots are needed to fly planes. As it is, pilots have already ceded much of the control of their airplanes to algorithms. Nothing sadly demonstrates this better than the two recent crashes of the Boeing 737 MAX planes, killing hundreds of people. In both cases, once the pilots realized the planes were stalling, they tried to take over control of the planes but were unable to do so. There was clearly an error in the programming of the planes, which caused the planes to act as they did under certain conditions. The 737 MAX planes were grounded worldwide after the second crash. At that time of the grounding, the 737 MAX planes had flown over 41,000 flights, carrying more than 6.5 million passengers. The planes are now being rectified with more rigorous testing and should soon be back in the air safer than before.[13]

While the 737 MAX plane crashes, were caused by faulty programming, 80 per cent of all crashes have been caused by pilot error.[14] There has been at least one case of a pilot wilfully crashing a plane into a mountain. In March 2015, Andreas Lubitz, a co-pilot with Germanwings, a subsidiary of Lufthansa, who had previously been treated for suicidal tendencies, locked the pilot out of the cockpit and drove the plane into a mountainside in France, killing all 150 people on board.[15] Automated planes will not suffer from pilot errors, nor have suicidal tendencies and drive planes into mountainsides.

There are other modes of transport, straight out of science fiction comics that are fast becoming reality. Hyperloop travel, drone ships, journeys to the moon and human settlements on Mars are all coming much sooner than we could ever have imagined a few years ago. This takes us back to Elon Musk, the man behind the Tesla electric and self-driving cars. Other entities are also working towards some of these goals, but no other entity is as far ahead in any of these spheres as Elon Musk.

On 5 December 2019, SpaceX, a company started by Elon Musk in 2009, launched a Falcon rocket (named after a spaceship from the movie *Star Wars*) to resupply the International Space Station (IIS).[16, 17] A few minutes after the launch, the second stage of the Falcon rocket separated and the first stage returned to land in the Atlantic Ocean, on an automated spaceport drone ship (ASDS), named by Musk as, 'Of Course I Still Love You', after a spaceship commanded by artificial intelligences, from a science fiction novel, *The Player of Games*, written by the late Iain M. Banks. Other ASDS ships in the fleet are also named after spaceships from the same author. The second stage of the Falcon rocket released the spacecraft Dragon, which docked with the ISS. Dragon was named by Musk after the song 'Puff the Magic Dragon' by Peter, Paul and Mary, reportedly as a response to critics who considered his space flight projects impossible.[18] The Falcon is scheduled to stay docked with the ISS for a month after which it will return to the earth with the results of various experiments being carried out on the ISS. Different versions of Dragon are designed to carry both cargo and humans and can carry up to seven people. On 31 May 2020, a Dragon spacecraft carrying two astronauts docked with the ISS.

On 19 December 2019, Boeing attempted to send up its Starliner spacecraft to rendezvous with the ISS. The attempt was a failure. This was a major setback for Boeing as well as NASA, as NASA had contracted with Boeing to be a second contractor by paying Boeing a rate which was 60 per cent more than what it paid SpaceX.

Elon Musk started SpaceX with the avowed purpose of eventually setting up a human colony on Mars. He is getting there. SpaceX is developing its Starship spacecraft and Super Heavy rocket (collectively referred to as Starship). The Starship can fly to an earth orbit on its own and be refuelled there to be able to reach Mars with a cargo in excess of 150 tons, or with about sixty humans, along with their supplies. The plans for Martian colonization are not of the distant future. Musk intends to send two Starships laden with solar panels, mining equipment and other supplies, including food to Mars in 2022. In 2024 (Mars is the closest to the earth about every two years. This is known as the synodic period), he plans to send four Starships to Mars, two with supplies and two carrying about sixty humans each. Unlike the moon landings of fifty years ago, these will be permanent human settlements. For the first time, we would become a multiplanetary species. We, and the plants we grow on Mars, will represent the only known life forms to exist anywhere other than the earth. I must admit that I am a little bewildered at the lack of media attention and general excitement leading up to such a momentous event.[19, 20] Musk is intending to retire the Falcon rocket and replace it with the Super Heavy rocket and the Starship as his main workhorse to be able to concentrate on one vehicle. Apart from working in space and going to the moon and Mars, it will also be able to take a spaceship load of people from any place on the earth to any other in about half an hour.

Another new mode of transport being explored is a Hyperloop system. Imagine, the year is 2030 and you're in a sleek pod-like capsule that is levitating inside a low-pressure steel tube travelling at over 600 mph or over a thousand kilometres per hour. This is Hyperloop, the futuristic transportation method, first pitched by Elon Musk in 2012.[21]

Elon Musk may have dreamt up the Hyperloop, but most of the developmental work on it has so far been carried out by others. SpaceX, Musk's company had, until recently, largely limited itself to holding competitions for the design and speed trials of the pods which are to travel in the Hyperloop. The 2019 trials were won by a team from the Technical University of Munich who clocked a speed of 463 kilometres per hour over the length of a mile-long (1.6-kilometre) tunnel. Musk has promised a 10-kilometre-long vacuum tube-like tunnel for the 2020 competition. The tunnel will have a diameter of 12 feet and will presumably be built by Musk's Boring Company, which bores tunnels, with help from SpaceX. To build such a tunnel in one year would, by itself, be a minor engineering miracle. SpaceX's new hyperloop test facilities will be at or very near full-scale relative to the operational, human-rated transportation system that is the concept's ultimate goal.[22]

Meanwhile, other companies, notably Richard Branson's Virgin Hyperloop One, Hyperloop Transportation Technologies, Arrivo and Transpod, are all progressing. Virgin Hyperloop One appears to be ahead of the field, having completed its phase two trials. It has already entered into agreements to construct a few Hyperloops in some places across the world, including one from Mumbai to Pune, to cover the distance in half an hour. In October 2019, Virgin Hyperloop announced it would begin construction of a facility in north Texas. The Hyperloop routes in Texas plan to take travellers from Dallas-Fort Worth to Laredo in about forty-five minutes, Dallas-Fort Worth to Austin in about seventeen minutes and Dallas-Fort Worth to San Antonio in twenty-five minutes.[23,24] Musk's Boring Company is planning to dig a Hyperloop tunnel that would make it possible to travel from Washington DC to New York City in a half an hour.[25] The sense I get is that the age of the railway construction boom times is coming again. Many individual Hyperloops will be laid out to be eventually connected into continent-wide networks.

The Boring Company is an infrastructure and tunnel construction company, founded by Elon Musk in December 2016, initially as a subsidiary of SpaceX and became an independent company in 2018. Musk has cited difficulty with the Los Angeles traffic, which he said was 2D in nature. He envisaged boring multilevel tunnels and speeding up traffic flow through them. This is not to be confused with the hyperloop system. This is like an intracity tram service as against the hyperloop being an intercity train service. Only both will be in tunnels. The top speed of this service will be slower too, at about 200 kilometres per hour. The Boring Company is designing its own tunnel-boring machine, which is expected to be fifteen times faster than the state-of-the-art machines in 2017. The Boring Company will bore the tunnels for both the systems.[26]

In the introduction to this book, I had written about the Iridium project in which seventy-seven satellites were in the process of being launched to provide a worldwide communication network, but which was overtaken by the advent of the cell phones. Events, it now seems, are coming full circle around. Technology has moved on. Starlink is a satellite constellation being constructed by Elon Musk's SpaceX. It started launching its operational satellites on 24 May 2019, when it launched sixty satellites. It followed up with another sixty satellites on 11 November 2019. As of November 2019, they had deployed 122 satellites and were planning to deploy sixty more per launch at a rate of one launch every two weeks. In total, nearly 12,000 satellites will be deployed by the mid 2020s, with a possible later extension to 42,000 satellites.

These will be small mass-produced satellites, capable of providing connectivity directly into individual homes and other premises through a pizza box size receiver.[27] We may see the end of ungainly and radiating cell towers. It will become possible for a person anywhere on earth to communicate with another. With an increasing number of smartphones being able to download translation apps, mankind will revert to the days before it was confounded when building the biblical tower of Babel. SpaceX may not be the only company putting up satellites. In December 2019, Bloomberg's Mark Gurman reported that Apple has a secret team working on new satellite wireless and data technologies to send data to its devices through its own satellite network.[28]

It would appear that Elon Musk has never lost focus of his early dream of establishing a human colony on Mars. He believes that humankind must expand beyond the earth to safeguard its survival in the event of any catastrophe, either natural, such as an asteroid strike or a super volcano, or man-made, such as an atomic conflagration or the inadvertent creation of a virus or the triggering of a mini black hole. In 2001, he tried to buy a decommissioned intercontinental ballistic missile (ICBM) from Russia for a project to land a miniature experimental greenhouse on Mars, growing crops on Martian regolith (a kind of broken rock soil prevalent on both the moon and on Mars). Being unable to buy one, he decided to build it himself and started SpaceX. In Ashlee Vance's biography, Musk stated that he wants to establish a Mars colony by 2040, with a population of 80,000. Musk stated that, since Mars' atmosphere lacks oxygen, all transportation would have to be electric[29] (electric cars, electric trains, Hyperloop). Tesla's Solar City is now among the largest manufacturers of solar panels. In a joint venture with Panasonic, Musk has established the Gigafactory, the largest manufacturer of lithium-ion battery devices.[30] His interests encompass these very fields. The expertise of his Boring Company, it has been conjectured, would be put to use in creating underground living spaces on Mars to protect from radiation and to create an earth-like atmosphere. Starlink's expertise will be needed to put communication satellites around Mars and also in heliocentric orbits if a Martian colony is to stay in constant communication with the earth. Whatever his motivations, Musk has been and is likely to continue being a major contributor to the changing profile of our transport solutions.

Electric cars, self-driving cars, flying cars, drone aircraft and ships, Hyperloops, trams in tunnels, human settlements on the moon and Mars, have all moved from the science fiction world into the real world during the last ten years. During the next ten years, all of these will move towards maturity. The world then will be as well connected as it is possible for it to be. Every human on earth will have the technological ability to interact with any other human being. And what after that? If new ideas keep arising and being implemented, not only in the fields of transportation and connectivity but other fields as well, I can only revert to the words of President Ronald Reagan, in his address to the nation on 5 November 1984, 'You ain't seen nothin' yet.'

It is not with any great clarity that we can look at the consequences arising out of individual worldwide connectivity, easier space travel and human settlements on the moon and Mars. It is too early for that. All we can say with certainty is that new opportunities and if not threats, problems that are over and above what we can visualize today will surely arise. The consequences arising out of autonomously driven electric cars, flying cars, aircraft, ships, Hyperloops and trams in tunnels are easier to imagine.

Desirable Consequences:

1. Transportation will increasingly shift to being electric-driven. This will start limiting the emission of carbon dioxide, soot and other particulate matter, slowing down global warming and leading to a cleaner environment.
2. Getting from one place to another will become faster and cheaper.

Worrisome Consequences:

1. Along with automated cars, other means of transport will also become automated.
2. The newer modes of transport, such as flying cars and the Hyperloop will require reaction times that are much too quick for human reflexes. The option to have them manned by humans simply will not exist. This will lead to a massive loss of jobs currently existing in the transport sector.

6

WATER PURIFICATION AND DESALINATION

A new paper, which comes from the European Commission's Joint Research Centre (JRC), paints a disturbing picture of a nearby future where people are fighting over access to water. A water conflict database lists 551 such historical flare-ups. The researchers put such chances at 75 to 95 per cent in the next fifty to 100 years.[1] There has been speculation that water could be the cause of a third world war. But it need not be so.

There is no shortage of water in the world. Nearly three-fourths of our planet is covered in water and ice. The shortage is of clean fresh water, which can be used for drinking, domestic purposes and for agriculture. A mere 0.014 per cent of all water on the earth is both fresh and easily accessible. Of the remaining, 97 per cent is saline and a little less than 3 per cent is hard to access, most of it in the form of ice.

The fresh water that is available is not evenly distributed, with the result that while some places have adequate or more than adequate water, other places are often prone to either droughts or floods. This uneven distribution of water is likely to be further exacerbated with changing and more volatile weather patterns attributed to global warming and the resultant extreme weather events. Scarcely a year goes by without some places reporting the driest, wettest, hottest or coldest year in a century or more.

Rising populations in some parts of the world, along with rising standards of living, will put increasing stress on water supplies. Currently, more than half the world's population or about

4 billion people live under conditions of severe water scarcity for at least one month in a year. Half a billion people in the world face severe water scarcity all year round. Half of the world's largest cities experience water scarcity. Demand for water is expected to outstrip supply by 40 per cent in 2030 if current trends continue.[2] Such a situation is untenable. Solutions will need to be sought. Fortunately, solutions are in sight.

We have known for a long time that seawater can be desalinated. Earlier, desalination was done through different types of distillation. Some of the methods were solar distillation, vacuum distillation, multistage flash distillation and vapour-compression distillation. Reverse osmosis (RO) was first discovered in the 1950s by researchers at the University of California at Los Angeles and the University of Florida, but the flux was too low to be commercially viable. Osmosis is a process where if two solutions, of different concentrations, are separated by a semipermeable membrane, the solvent moves through the membrane from the less concentrated solution to the more concentrated one until the concentrations are equal. This is the process that makes the bringing and pickling of vegetables possible. Reverse osmosis is the process where seawater or any other solution is made to flow, under pressure, through a suitable membrane in the opposite direction to normal osmotic flow. This effectively strains out the solute. In the case of seawater, the water molecules are pumped through the membrane, but the larger salt molecules and other contaminants are prevented from going through.[3] Reverse osmosis is essentially a sieving process under pressure. It is through a very fine sieve, under fairly high pressure.

It takes energy to desalinate seawater. Different methods of desalination use differing amounts of energy. RO is by far the most efficient. The total equivalent electrical energy to desalinate one cubic metre of water, measured in kilowatt hours (kWh/m^3), in 2013, by some of the methods was: multistage flash distillation: 13.5–25.5; multi-effect distillation: 6.5–11; mechanical vapor compression distillation: 7–12; RO filtration: 3–5.5.

By 2019, the energy requirement for desalination by RO had dropped to 2.5–3.5 kWh/m^3. That is an average of 3 kWh/m^3. Let us put that energy requirement into perspective. An average American family uses 1000 litres or one metric ton of water per day. We have seen in the chapter on energy that the price of solar generated-electric power has dropped to below two US cents per kWh. (Recall the Los Angeles PPA). If an average American family were to have all its water needs met by desalinated seawater, the energy cost would only be about six cents per day. While an average individual American consumes 378 litres per day, an average European consumes 189 litres, and an average African only 57 litres. The UN recommends a minimum water availability of 49 litres per person per day.[4, 5] The energy cost of desalinating 49 litres works out to a daily cost of a third of a US cent.

The drop in the energy cost of desalinating seawater has been mainly because of improvements in the membranes through which the seawater is pumped to remove the salt dissolved in it and to some extent, improvements in the pumps. The cost is expected to come down further because of an entirely new class of material called Metal Organic Frameworks (MOF).

Researchers are working on honeycombed-patterned MOF membranes only a few atoms thick, which can desalinate seawater, using far less energy than current RO membranes.[6] MOFs were discovered at the end of the twentieth Century. They are a versatile class of materials, which can be designed for a multitude of specific applications, including seawater desalination. Such materials are referred to as different frameworks. Having captured chemists' imagination, researchers would create more than 20,000 different frameworks over the next two decades. With around 1,000 research papers still being published every year, there seems to be no end to chemists' love affair with MOFs.[7]

MOFs are crystals that act as sponges due to their vast internal surfaces—the largest of any known substance. They are, therefore, ideal for capturing, storing and removing or releasing compounds such as ions and salt that render seawater undrinkable. Professor Huanting Wang of the Monash University faculty in Melbourne, Australia and his team have discovered that MOF membranes can act like the cell membranes of organic structures, taking on an ion-selective filtering function. This opens up the possibility of extracting different substances from seawater, including lithium, which is in high demand for making lithium-ion batteries, from the mineral-rich effluent brine that is the byproduct of seawater desalination.[8] There are many other minerals in seawater that are higher in concentration than lithium and others in lesser concentration. Gold is also present in seawater in trace quantities.[9] With the ability of MOFs to selectively capture different ions, it is possible that the desalination of seawater could become a profitable mining operation with fresh water becoming a byproduct. The RO effluent is today considered to be a polluting byproduct, but it may well turn out to be a valuable raw material.

Asked, when we might expect MOFs to be used extensively, Professor Wang replied, 'We are working to scale up membrane fabrication, and then test the membrane under industrial-level conditions.' According to him, it could be between 2021 and 2023. Meanwhile, Physical Sciences Inc., an American company, has been awarded a contract from the US department of energy to demonstrate high-performance MOF-based desalination membranes that offer the potential to provide at least a 50 per cent reduction in energy use compared to current RO membranes for a system with controlled pore size.[10]

With the doubling of the efficiency of the desalination process and the likely halving of the cost of solar and wind energy in the next few years, the energy cost of desalinated seawater could be between one and two US cents per metric ton. The energy cost of desalinating water depends upon the amount of salt dissolved in the water. The lesser the salt dissolved in it the lesser the amount of energy needed to desalinate it. Seawater has the highest concentration of salts among readily available water sources. Salinity is measured as the Total Dissolved Solids (TDS) and varies in oceans from 35 grams per litre (g/L) to 45 g/L. Brackish water typically has concentrations of 1 to 10 g/L.[11] If the source of water is brackish water, it will be that much cheaper to convert into drinking water. Water shortage is something we will manage nicely, provided there is water available. Any kind of water will do. It could be seawater, brackish water or plain dirty water.

We have so far discussed only the cost of energy to desalinate 1 metric ton of water. There are other costs involved, such as the capital cost of setting up the desalination plant, its maintenance cost, operating costs, including labour cost and the cost of the piping to take the seawater from the sea, the piping to dispose the brine in an ecologically sustainable manner and finally, to pipe the fresh water to individual homes or other destinations.

After taking account of all the costs, the cost of one cubic metre of desalinated seawater has already dropped to below fifty US cents.[12] The cost of power accounts for almost half the operating cost of desalinating seawater.[13] With the anticipated improvements in generating electricity from wind and solar sources, the overall cost of desalinating seawater with energy from clean renewable energy should drop to below thirty US cents per cubic metre of drinking water in a few years. At this price, the cost of 49 litres per person per day, recommended by the UN, works out to be about one and a half US cents. This is affordable everywhere on the earth.

Renewable energy, whether solar or wind, is ideally suited for seawater desalination. The biggest drawback of solar and wind energy is that the energy is intermittent. To overcome this shortcoming, solar parks and wind farms have to operate in tandem with sources of energy that are capable of being quickly ramped up or dampened, such as hydroelectric power plants or gas-fired power plants, or they have to invest in battery banks as the back-up when energy is not being generated. This can be expensive. Desalination needs only to be carried out when renewable energy is being generated. In the case of seawater desalination, the only back-up required is large tanks or reservoirs to hold the desalinated water for when seawater is not being desalinated.

Another benefit of solar and wind energy is that they are not polluting and do not add to the carbon dioxide in the air. This is important because, with the present cost of fifty US cents a ton and an anticipated cost of thirty US cents a ton for large desalination plants, huge amounts of seawater will be desalinated. The world's first desalination plant with an output of over a million tons of fresh water a day is operational in Ras Al Khair in Saudi Arabia. The next five plants are all well over half a million tons per day.[14] The size of the desalination plants and their numbers will only keep increasing. The Ras Al Khair plant alone desalinates 1,036,000 cubic metres of water every day. That is enough water to meet all the water needs of one million and thirty-six thousand American families or of over twenty-one million individuals at 49 litres a day.

Once we have the desalinated water in our tanks or reservoirs, it has to reach people. Let us see where the people are. Presently, about 40 per cent of the world's population lives within 100 kilometres (60 miles) of a sea coast.[15] Most people live near an ocean or near a river with easy access to an ocean, rather than in the interior of a major land mass. In fact, approximately two-thirds of the world's population live within 500 kilometres (300 miles) of an ocean, and four-fifths live within 800 kilometres (500 miles).[16] These are distances to which a valuable resource like water can economically be pumped.

There are challenges, of course. The capital cost of setting up a desalination plant is high and poorer parts of the planet may find it difficult to fund the project. However, the anticipated cost of thirty US cents per cubic metre includes the amortized cost of capital. If populist governments do not try to give away the water for free, the entire project can fund itself, making affordable water available to almost every human, obviating the need for water wars.

Reverse osmosis or desalination of seawater is not the only route being explored to increasing our supply of fresh water. Cloud seeding to cause rain is also being experimented upon. The United Arab Emirates (UAE) is one of the countries at the forefront of this endeavour. Although cloud seeding is not yet an exact science, the process of shooting salt flares into clouds has increased by 15 to 25 per cent. According to Khalid Mohamed Al Obeidi, head of cloud seeding at the National Centre of Meteorology, it can sometimes go as high as 30 per cent. He adds that the UAE is deliberately inducing rain and cloud seeding will 'definitely help boost' the groundwater supply of a desert country with an average rainfall of only about 100 mm. More rainfall will help ease the water stress and cloud seeding is cheaper and costs one fil (about a third of a US cent) per cubic metre of water produced as compared to sixty fils (twenty US cents) to desalinate the same amount of water and is more environment-friendly than desalination. He admits, 'We cannot control the rain and we cannot control the cloud because it is always moving, but we can study each cloud formation and see if it is suitable for cloud seeding.'[17]

The cost of desalinated seawater, or cloud seeding induced rainwater will then be at a level where it can be used for agriculture, provided water is not used wastefully. Some countries, notably Israel, already practise this method of agriculture. Other places where water is limited can learn from best practices worldwide and have thriving farmlands, in what was once arid or even desert land.

For me, another science fiction fantasy is becoming reality. The deserts will turn green. Staying true to science fiction, these new farms will not look like the rolling farmlands we see today. They will be automated to a large extent and may not even need soil but grow on hydroponics and aeroponics, consuming as little water as possible. We will look closer at this in the next chapter.

Desirable Consequences:

1. Water stress will disappear from most parts of the world.
2. This will lead to better hygiene and hence, better health and increasing longevity.
3. Increased water supply and more efficient agricultural practices will mean more food. Hunger may become a thing of the past.
4. If and when the use of MOFs becomes widespread for the desalination of seawater, we will have more access to a wide range of minerals, including for fertilizers.

Worrisome Consequences:

1. Happily, there are no worrisome consequences for an increased supply of clean fresh water, except for a distant possibility. As we become more proficient in a form of agriculture, which needs reduced water and labour, we will shift to the new ways of agriculture everywhere. This will lead to a displacement of farm jobs, which are a major component of total jobs in many developing countries.

7

AGRICULTURE AND MEAT PRODUCTION

Singapore is a small country. Its area is 721.5 square kilometres and its population is 5.831 million. It, therefore, has a population density of 7804 people per square kilometre. It is the country with the highest population density of any country in the world, if we ignore the tiny principality of Monaco, which is all of two square kilometres in area. With its limited area and high population density, Singapore, not surprisingly, imports over 90 per cent of its food. In 2016, Singapore produced 22,458 tons of vegetables, while its population consumed 524,462 tons of them. That is, it grew only 4.28 per cent of its needs.[1]

In March 2019, the government of Singapore set the '30 by 30' goal, by which it aims to become 30 per cent self-sufficient in food production by the year 2030. By 2030, its population is expected to rise to 6.34 million and its population density increase to 8,787 persons per square kilometre. How does Singapore plan to achieve its ambitious goal? Singapore has little land, hardly any surplus or idle labour and already recycles 40 per cent and desalinates seawater to the extent of 30 per cent to meet its water needs. Singapore can only meet its target by embracing new developments in agricultural technology.

For those of us who grew up in the 1950s and equated agriculture with farmland and farmers tilling fields with the help of oxen and understood the seasonal rotation of crops, the new developments in agriculture technology are not short of being magical. The new ways of growing agricultural produce are already delivering abundant yields, as much as ten to fifteen times as much from the same land area as in traditional farming, using as little as 2 per cent of the water as before, with zero pesticides and only 40 per cent of earlier fertilizer usage. Furthermore, these systems ignore the seasons completely and grow the crops around the year. They are not even dependent on sunlight for plant growth, but supply the light through LED lighting of the exact wavelengths needed by the plants. Plants are now propagated without resorting to the randomness of pollination and seeds. The soil quality does not matter either. Plants can now be grown without any soil at all.

Announcing the ambitious '30 by 30' goal, environment and water resources minister, Masagos Zulkifli, told Parliament that this calls for new solutions to raise productivity. Technologies such as indoor multistorey LED-lit vegetable farms and indoor multistorey recirculating aquaculture systems can produce ten to fifteen times more than traditional outfits. And high-tech farms can be less labour intensive as well. 'Farmers of the future will operate computerized central systems in a pleasant environment,' Mr Masagos said. Singapore is not only relying on new agriculture technologies to increase efficiencies but also automating fairly complex operations where it can. One local first mover is Barramundi Asia, which uses large sea cages to farm fish. Using technology, it can vaccinate 9,000 fish in an hour, a far cry from the 600 fish an hour if by hand. N&N Agriculture, an egg farm, uses a fully automated system for crate washing, packing eggs and wrapping egg trays, saving thousands of man-hours.

The Intergovernmental Panel on Climate Change estimates widespread declines in crop yields of up to a quarter by 2050 due to global warming. Singapore, which imports most of its food, wants to be less vulnerable to the volatility of the global food market.[2] The same logic applies to other countries as well. It may one day be imperative to have food production systems that are impervious to changing climate patterns. Singapore may be the first country to have announced a national goal of developing and establishing the new agriculture systems, but it is not the only country which is pursuing them.

The farming I witnessed growing up in the 1950s in India was traditional farming and had been going on in much the same way for over a thousand years. It was prevalent in most developing countries at the time. The more developed parts of the world had shifted to what we called mechanized farming, which used tractors and combine harvesters and where farm hands were replaced by machines. Our textbooks told us that about half of all Indians were engaged in agriculture. We were amazed to learn that the equivalent figure for countries with mechanized farming was only between 2 and 5 per cent.

Traditional farming has all but vanished and mechanized farming has evolved much further from where it then was. Before we see what new heights mechanized farming has reached, let us first look at the new kind of farming, which is rapidly emerging. This new farming does not yet have a generic name. Perhaps, Smart Farming is an appropriate name. While these new farming techniques have many forms, including hydroponics, aquaponics, aeroponics and vertical farming, I suggest the name Smart Farming because they all have one thing in common. They increasingly rely on multiple sensors and algorithms to carry out their plant tending operations with little input from humans.

Hydroponics is the concept and practice of growing plants without soil. Inert material such as stone aggregate or gravel is used to give physical support to the plants. All the nutritional needs of the plants are delivered through a water solution into which fertilizer and other nutrients have been dissolved. This solution is periodically flooded and drained from the root area of the plants, providing both nutrition and aeration of the roots. Hydroponics in a primitive sort of a way is thousands of years old. The famous Hanging Gardens of Babylon, in around 6000 BCE, are the earliest record of hydroponics. Since the region's climate was dry and rarely saw rain, people believe that the ancient Babylonians used a chain-pull system for watering garden plants.

In this method, water was pulled from the river and flowed up along the chain system and dropped to the steps or landing of the garden. There are other historical examples of crude hydroponics, but the modern practice of hydroponics can be said to have started in the early 1930s, when W.F. Gericke, of the University of California at Berkeley, experimented with nutriculture for the production of agricultural crops. He publicized his findings but was largely met with scepticism.

The earliest well-known application of hydroponic plant cultivation was in the early 1940s when hydroponics was used on Wake Island, a soilless island in the Pacific Ocean. This island was used as a refuelling stop for Pan American Airlines. The lack of soil meant that it was impossible to grow anything using traditional practices and it was incredibly expensive to airlift fresh vegetables. Hydroponics solved the issues exceedingly well and provided fresh vegetables for all the troops on this distant island. After the war, hydroponic cultivation was still used widely by the military. In the 1950s, the soilless method of agriculture expanded to a variety of countries, including England, France, Italy, Spain, Sweden, the USSR and Israel.[3]

Stone aggregate or other inert material is used in hydroponics to physically support the root system of plants. The support material provides no nutrition to the plants. The nutrition for the plants is provided by water into which fertilizers have been dissolved. This is periodically let into the root system and then drained out. This practice provides for both the nutritional needs of the plant as well as the aeration of the roots. There are two kinds of hydroponic systems, open and closed. In the open system, once the fertilizer and water are mixed, the mixture is led into the root system a few times and then discarded. In the closed system, as the water and fertilizers are taken up by the plants, more water and fertilizer are added to the existing mixture as required. This avoids wastage of both water and fertilizers. As can be imagined, the closed system is more efficient. It uses only

15 per cent of the water used in regular farming, with much less fertilizer and a productivity increase of two and a half times.[4]

Although hydroponics is mostly used to grow vegetables and leafy herbs and plants, Emirati farmer, Saleh Al Mansouri, has taken to growing rice through hydroponics in water-scarce UAE. As the water is recycled, its consumption is far less than the water wasteful traditional rice farming. Yields for a given area are also higher than in the waterlogged paddy fields of Southeast Asia or the Indian subcontinent. Mr Saleh has also used hydroponics to produce oranges, grapes, pineapples and papayas.[5] There is no theoretical limit to what can be grown hydroponically.

Aeroponics is a more efficient form of hydroponics. There is no stone aggregate to provide support for the roots. Instead, the roots are pushed inside apertures in pipes and the pipes are pumped with a fine mist of water and all the required nutrients. This method provides the plant roots with a constant supply of both nutrients and aeration. The pipes can be in any configuration, horizontal or vertical. This makes vertical farms growing inside tall buildings possible.

It was NASA that first carried out pioneering research on aeroponics in the 1990s, when it was looking for techniques to grow plants in space. According to NASA, 'Aeroponics systems can reduce water usage by 98 per cent, fertilizer usage by 60 per cent and pesticide usage by a 100 per cent, while maximizing crop yields. Crops grown in the aeroponic systems have also been shown to uptake more minerals and vitamins, making the plants healthier and potentially more nutritious.' About tomatoes, it says, 'Using an aeroponic system, growers can start the plants in a growing chamber, then transplant them just ten days later. This advanced technology produces six crop cycles per year, instead of the traditional one to two crop cycles.'[6, 7]

Aquaponics is about growing fish and vegetables in one combined ecosystem. In this system, a fish tank and a hydroponic system work together in a symbiotic relation with benefits to both. The main input into the system is fish food for the fish. As the fish eat, grow and multiply, they release excretions into the water, increasing its toxicity. In a stand-alone fish tank, this water needs to be replaced frequently. In an aquaponics system, the water with the fish wastes in it is led to the hydroponic part of the system, where the wastes are broken down by the nitrifying bacteria initially into nitrites and subsequently into nitrates that are utilized by the plants as nutrients. The water, in turn, gets filtered in the roots of the plants and the aggregate supporting the roots before being returned to the fish tank.

As existing hydroponic and aquaculture farming techniques form the basis for all aquaponic systems, the size, complexity and types of foods grown in an aquaponic system can vary as much as any system found in either distinct farming system. There is considerable saving of water as well of fertilizer for the plants. There is an 80 to 90 per cent less consumption of water than if the fish keeping and farming had been independent systems. The only water added is to replace the water lost due to absorption and transpiration by plants. In a well-matched aquaponics system, fertilizer availability is adequate. Only some minerals and micronutrients need to be added to optimize plant growth and yield.

There is growing worldwide interest in aquaponics, ranging from the hobbyist to the commercial farming companies. A 3.75 acres aquaponics facility that claims to be the first indoor salmon farm in the US also includes automated technology. At the other end of the spectrum, an Atlanta company called Earth Solutions sells aquaponics kits online. The kits range in price from USD 268 to USD 3,000, and come with pipes and pumps, frames and fittings. If these trends continue, the pressure on the depleting stocks of fish in the oceans should ease considerably.[8, 9]

Vertical farming is the growing of plants in many levels, one above the other. Vertical farming is compatible with all three emerging trends of intense or high-density and high-yielding technologies discussed above, namely, hydroponics, aeroponics and aquaponics. In the case of aquaponics, the fish tank is at ground level while the hydroponic part is on multiple levels above it. Vertical farming is fast gaining popularity and for good reason. It offers several advantages.

Dr Dickson Despommier, emeritus professor of public and environmental health at Columbia University, challenged his class of graduate students in 1999 to come up with a design to grow plants on multiple layers. Despommier and his students then proposed a design of a thirty-storey vertical farm equipped with artificial lighting, advanced hydroponics and aeroponics that could produce enough food for 50,000 people. They further outlined that approximately hundred kinds of fruits and vegetables would grow on the upper floors while lower floors would house chicken and fish subsisting on the plant waste. Although Despommier's skyscraper farm has not yet been built, it popularized the concept of vertical farming and inspired many other designs that have been built. As the concept keeps proving itself, larger ones are sure to be built and have been specifically mentioned by the Singaporean minister who unveiled the '30 by 30' plan in Parliament.

Vertical farming has another add-on to it known as controlled environment agriculture. Here, as the name suggests, the entire environment, including air, temperature, light, water, humidity, carbon dioxide and plant nutrition, is controlled. The very quality of light for plants can be made better than sunlight.[10]

Chlorophyll A, which is present in all photosynthetic organisms, absorbs blue light with a wavelength of 430 nanometres (nm) and red light of 662 nm. Chlorophyll B, which is similar to chlorophyll A, exists in green algae and plants and absorbs light of 453 nm and 642 nm and helps plants absorb a more extensive range of light wavelengths. Green light is not absorbed by plants but reflects back, making the plants look green to us.[11] We have had green and red LED lights from the 1960s, when LED lights first emerged. It was not until 1989 that diodes emitting blue light were finally invented. With the three prime colours now available, it was possible to generate any colour and hence the wavelength of light. Witness the multitude of hues on LED television screens.[12]

It is now possible to bathe any variety of plant with the exact wavelengths of light needed by it. There is no need to waste energy by giving it light it cannot use.

With the complete control of the environment available, it is now possible to locate vertical farming anywhere.[12] It could be in abandoned factories, warehouses or even abandoned mineshafts, shipping containers or for that matter on the moon or Mars. New buildings can also be designed, where humans and plants can cohabit it to mutual benefit. The oxygen that plants release during photosynthesis is beneficial to humans and the carbon dioxide we release is good for the plants. It is also pleasant to live or work in green surroundings.

Traditional farming's arable land requirements are too large and invasive to remain sustainable for the growing population of future generations. Vertical farming allows for, in some cases, over ten times the crop yield per acre than traditional farming. All-season farming further multiplies the productivity of the farmed surface by four to six times. With crops such as strawberries, it could be as high as thirty times. Vertical farming also allows for production of a larger variety of harvestable crops because of its ability to isolate crops into different sections. It enables a multitude of different crops to be grown and harvested at once.

The big disadvantage of all forms of modern farming, especially vertical farming, is that they are capital-intensive to start up and consume more energy to run than traditional farming does. Part of the energy consumption can be set off against transportation energy usage, as these modern systems can be situated within or very close to major population centres. There are differing opinions regarding the financial viability of these systems. The debate, I believe, can be put to rest with one case in Singapore. In 2012, the world's first commercial vertical farm was opened there by Sky Green Farms and is three storeys high. They currently have over a hundred nine-metre tall towers. They would not be building so many vertical-farming towers if it were not financially viable.

Aerofarms is an American company that runs vertical farms using aeroponics and are building the world's largest vertical farm. Their systems use 95 per cent less water than field-farmed food and with yields 390 times higher per square foot annually. They use no pesticides.[13] There are many vertical farms being set up across the world in all sorts of places, including disused factories and warehouses, mineshafts and tunnels. Shipping containers are becoming a popular place to put these systems in.

In 2016, a start-up called Local Roots launched the 'TerraFarm', a vertical farming system hosted in a 40-foot shipping container, which includes computer vision integrated with an artificial neural network to monitor the plants; it is remotely monitored from California. It is claimed that the TerraFarm system 'has achieved cost parity with traditional, outdoor farming' with each unit producing the equivalent of 'three to five acres of farmland', using 97 per cent less water through water recapture and harvesting the evaporated water through air conditioning.[14]

In another development, the way we propagate plants has changed. It is no longer solely dependent on bees and the cross-fertilization of plants with the attendant uncertainty of the quality of the next generation. The development is tissue culture. This is the in vitro aseptic culture of cells, tissues, organs or whole plants under controlled nutritional and environmental conditions, often to produce the clones of plants. The resultant clones are true to type of the selected genotype. In other words, an individual plant that has the wanted characteristics, which could include, fruit yield, resistance to disease, tolerance of drought or brackish water or any other desirable quality, can be multiplied hundreds and thousands of times, without exposing the next generation to the randomness of pollination or the trouble of harvesting seeds and replanting them.[15]

To sum it up, the new agricultural systems of hydroponics, aeroponics and aquaponics, increasingly coupled with vertical farming, are already delivering well over ten times the food per unit area than traditional farming, using as little as 3 per cent of the water. The food these systems deliver is of superior nutritional quality and is free of any pesticide or herbicide. To monitor and manage these complex systems, more AI and automation is employed, resulting in less manpower needed. These systems can be situated anywhere, requiring neither arable soil nor sunlight.

Let us now look at the developments taking place in traditional farming. There are two main areas that are being worked upon to significantly improve the efficiency and productivity of farms. One is automation with multiple sensors and cameras to gauge the current status of soil moisture, pest activity and other parameters and to then take remedial action. The other is the harnessing of microbes to do the tasks previously being done by chemicals.

Agriculture in the modern age is changing rapidly. The rising global population is creating a need for more agricultural produce. Farmers, meanwhile, are encountering labour shortages and higher farm wages. This is not new. For all of human history, increasing agricultural production has been a function of either adding more labourers or finding more efficient tools to do the job. It is no different now. In the face of labour shortages, farmers are turning to technology to make farms more efficient and automate the crop production cycle. To meet this demand, a growing number of agriculture tech start-ups are being started and funded.

These start-ups are addressing every aspect of the agriculture value chain. Some place remote sensors in the field to collect data about growing conditions. Others create software to manage seeds, soil, fertilizers and irrigation, and make predictions about timing and yield. Some start-ups use drones to monitor conditions remotely and even apply fertilizers, pesticides and other treatments from above. A growing cohort of companies are working on agricultural robotics to build automated tractors, combines and even fruit- and vegetable-picking robots. The large number of sensors and farm machinery, including tractors, irrigation systems, fertilizer and pesticide machines, and harvesting machines, are all interconnected by the Internet of Things (IoT), and guided by algorithms to conduct farming operations.[16] These systems are not yet perfect. They are growing in both their sophistication and reliability. They are also growing in number. By the end of the 2020s, automated farms are likely, in some countries at least, to be the norm rather than the exception.

In 2018, a project called the Hands-free Hectare completed its second wheat harvest. The project was run by UK's Harper Adams University and Precision Decisions and funded by the Agriculture and Horticulture Board and involved drilling, seeding, tending and harvesting a crop without operators on the machines and without any humans stepping on the field in one hectare of land. The performance of the team and the harvest yield improved in their second attempt, yielding a respectable harvest of 6.5 tons. The results are so encouraging that the project is now expanding to 35 hectares.[17]

In yet another advance, microbes and fungi are being actively developed to aid agriculture. Nitrogen is an essential component of all life. Our atmosphere is over 78 per cent nitrogen. The trouble is that atmospheric nitrogen is inert and cannot be directly used by us. To be of use to life, it must be fixated in the soil in the form of water-soluble nitrous compounds where it can be taken up by the plants. There are a few ways this happens in nature. Nitrogen can be fixed by lightning that converts nitrogen and oxygen into nitrogen oxides which seep into the soil where it makes nitrates which is of use to plants. Nitrogen-fixing is also carried out by some microorganisms such as azotobacter and archaea. Some nitrogen-fixing bacteria have symbiotic relationships with plant groups, especially legumes including peanuts.[18]

The natural addition of usable nitrogen into soil is not even nearly enough to grow the food we need for the world's burgeoning population. From the start of the twentieth century, we have augmented the natural supply of nitrogen through industrially produced fertilizers. In a sense, we are now going back to nature. Microbes and fungi are being actively developed to aid agriculture. In 2013, a consortium called BioAg Alliance was formed between Monsanto and Novozymes, a Danish firm, and it has a dozen microbe-based products in the market. These include fungicides, insecticides and bugs that liberate nitrogen, phosphorus and potassium compounds from the soil, making them soluble and thus, easier for plants to take up.

Similarly, in 2015, Syngenta and DSM, a Dutch company, formed a similar partnership. Also, in 2015, DuPont bought Taxon Biosciences, a Californian microbes firm. Hopeful start-ups abound. One such is Indigo in Boston. Its researchers are conducting field tests of some of its library of 40,000 microbes to see if they can alleviate the stress on cotton, maize, soya beans and wheat induced by drought and salinity. Another is Adaptive Symbiotic Technologies of Seattle. The scientists there study fungi that live symbiotically with plants. They believe they have found one, which confers salinity-resistance when transferred to crops such as rice.

The big prize, however, would be to persuade the roots of crops such as wheat to form partnerships with nitrogen-fixing soil bacteria. These would be similar to the natural partnerships formed with nitrogen-fixing bacteria and legumes. If wheat rhizomes could be persuaded, by genomic breeding or genome editing and splicing, to behave likewise, everyone except fertilizer companies would reap enormous benefits.[19, 20]

Let us now look at meats. The total meat production in the world has increased from about 70 million tons in 1961 to about 350 million tons in 2018. This figure excludes seafood and fish. As a global average, per capita meat consumption has increased from 23 kilograms in 1961 to around 43 kilograms in 2014. The global population has undergone rapid growth since the second half of the twentieth century but the growth in meat consumption has been almost double the population growth figure. This trend is expected to continue. Generally, the consumption of meat has increased with prosperity and rising incomes. Not all countries however fit into the same pattern. Meat consumption in China has grown fifteen-fold since 1961 and consumption in Brazil has quadrupled. The major exception to this pattern has been India—dominant lacto-vegetarian preferences mean that per capita meat consumption in 2013 was almost exactly the same as in 1961, at less than 4 kilograms per person. Per capita meat consumption varies widely from country to country and region to region. At 116 kilograms per capita, Australians are the largest meat consumers. The average European consumes nearly 80 kilograms, while the average North American, more than 110 kilograms.[21]

Growing meats is an expensive affair in terms of natural resources used, especially water, land and damage to the environment. The extensive use of antibiotics for meat production is largely responsible for the increasing strains of microbes that have become resistant to antibiotics, making it difficult to treat people infected by them.

An influential study in 2010 of the water footprint estimated that while vegetables had a footprint of about 322 litres per kilogram (l/kg) of produce, fruits drank up 962, meat was far more thirsty: chicken came in at 4,325 l/kg, pork at 5,988 l/kg, sheep/goat meat at 8,763 l/kg and beef at a stupendous 15,415 l/kg. Very little of this water is actually used by the animals to drink. Most of it is used to grow the crops to feed the animals. By some estimates, farming accounts for 70 per cent of the water used in the world today, but a 2013 study found that it uses up 92 per cent of our fresh water, with nearly one-third of that related to animal products.[22]

Livestock is the world's largest user of land resources, says the

UN Food and Agriculture Organization (FAO), 'with grazing land and crop land dedicated to the production of feed representing almost 80 per cent of all agricultural land. Feed crops are grown in one-third of total crop land, while the total land occupied by pasture is equivalent to 26 per cent of the ice-free terrestrial surface.'

Farms contribute to water pollution in a range of ways—some of those are associated more closely with arable farming, and some with livestock, but it is worth remembering that one-third of the world's grain is now fed to animals. The FAO believes that the livestock sector, which is growing and intensifying faster than crop production has 'serious implications' for water quality. The excess of nutrients and organic matter from fertilizers and animal excreta and leftover feed and crop, pathogens, metals, drug residues, hormones and feed additives, all contribute towards degradation of the environment.

According to the UN's Intergovernmental Panel on Climate Change, agriculture, forestry and other land use accounts for 24 per cent of greenhouse gases. It is difficult to apportion the exact amount contributed by animal farming. However, a 2017 landmark study found that the top three meat firms—JBS, Cargill and Tyson—emitted more greenhouse gases than all of France.[23]

If meat production uses up so much of the world's resources, how are we able to keep on increasing meat production? It is by turning to what can only be called, factory farming. Many, if not most, of us carry mental pictures of small family-run farms, growing some crops and keeping a mixture of farmyard animals like ducks, geese, hens, a few cows, along with a family dog or two, all growing up in sylvan surroundings and tended to by the farmer and his family. Alas, in many parts of the world, family farms are being increasingly replaced by factory farms.

Factory farms mimic the principles of mass production of the twentieth century applied to the industrial production of goods, such as cars and TVs. They focus on minimizing costs and maximizing profits. There are basically three ways in which costs can be minimized for growing animals. First is by reducing the land occupied by an animal, in other words, by crowding together as many animals as possible in a given space. Second is by preventing the movement of animals, so that energy is not wasted on foraging but used instead to maximize weight gain. This is further aided by the maximum use of growth hormones to enable the animals to further gain weight in the right places and enhance their market value. Crowded living spaces encourage the transmission of disease and make the enhanced use of antibiotics unavoidable.

Meat-producing facilities, such as factory farms and slaughterhouses, are far from humane, clean or sterile. Pigs in factory farms are confined to cages so small that they cannot even turn around. Chickens are kept in huge windowless sheds and cows are crammed together by the thousands in mud-and-faeces-filled feedlots. In slaughterhouses, animals are often scalded to death in feather or hair removal tanks or have their throats cut while still alive and struggling.[24] Other examples abound. The force-feeding of geese and ducks, with the purpose of fattening their livers for making foie gras, to the extent of ten times the normal size of their livers, is one such. Many places have banned the practice. While these practices may be unsettling, even abhorrent for some, there is no denying the fact that they have been economically successful. Since 1925, the average days to market for a US chicken has been reduced from 112 to forty-eight, while its weight has ballooned from a market weight of 2.5 pounds to 6.2 pounds.

I am a meat eater but live in India where a significantly large number of people are vegetarian and the only animal products they consume are milk and milk products. As a result, I have always been exposed to debates regarding the ethics of taking many lives to sustain one. I salved my conscience by telling myself that we have always, since we evolved, been an omnivorous species and ever since farming began, we have domesticated animals for the purpose of eating them. After becoming aware of modern animal rearing and slaughtering practices, it is becoming increasingly difficult to allay my sensibilities. Does this mean that we have a choice to either have the proteins our bodies need or have clear consciences? This may soon not be a choice we have to make. We can have both.

In 2013, Dutch stem cell researcher Mark Post unveiled the first lab-grown burger, handmade fibre-by-fibre from cow cells in petri dishes. He announced that the single-serving burger cost more than USD 300,000. At that cost, the burger was not a food option. It was a demonstration of a proof of the concept that such a thing could be done at all. But the research was promising enough for Post to launch a start-up called Mosa Meat to pursue making meat at scale. The company now says that its first products will be in the market by 2021, fuelled by a Series A fundraising round of USD 8.8 million announced in July 2018. It is targeting a burger price of USD 10. But it expects the price to continue to fall. 'We know where to improve the technology to get the price down,' Post says. Because many new start-ups are also working on the technology, progress could happen quickly. Cultured meat, also called clean meat, could theoretically be cheaper than meat from feedlots within a handful of years.

Since the first burger in 2013, the product has also improved. The company now cultures fat tissue, along with muscle tissue, to make the meat 'juicier and tastier'. The colour, taste and nutrition of the product has also improved and the company is continuing to further improve it.[25]

Lab-grown meat comes under many names—cultured meat, in vitro meat, synthetic meat and clean meat. It is not to be confused with a range of mock meats that already exist, such as soy turkey, vegan ham and meat-free beef. Lab-grown meats will be identical to natural meats, with the same proteins and nutritional values.

Lab-grown meat is made by growing muscle cells in a nutrient solution and encouraging them into muscle-like fibres. Simpler animal products, such as artificial milk or hen-free egg whites, can be created by yeast that has been genetically altered to produce the proteins found in milk or eggs. These proteins are then extracted and blended in the right amounts. Lab-grown meats are far more eco-friendly than regular meats. According to a study done by scientists from Oxford University and the University of Amsterdam, lab-grown meat produces 96 per cent fewer greenhouse gas emissions, and its creation requires up to 99 per cent less land, 96 per cent less water and 45 per cent less energy.[26]

The lab-grown meat industry is grappling with three challenges currently. These are taste, price and volume. Achieving a taste and texture that rivals real meat seems to be the easy bit. Compared with the first 2013 burger, scientists have already come a long way. In addition to incorporating fat cells and tissue, they have also learnt to increase the amount of flavour-giving proteins in the final product.

Marie Gibbons, a researcher from North Carolina State University working on cultured meat production, says there is no limit to what scientists could do with flavour. She thinks cultured meats could eventually be tastier than traditional meats. The first crop of cultured meats will inevitably take the form of burgers, nuggets, sausages and such. Unprocessed meat has a complex structure of bone, blood vessels, connective tissue and fat, and grows in specific shapes. Yet it should eventually be possible to grow complex tissue like this too, says Paul Mozdziak, Gibbons's colleague. He and scientists at various cellular agriculture organizations are keeping an eye on developments in regenerative medicine, the branch of biomedical science concerned with growing replacement organs. Regenerative medicine involves encouraging cells to grow on a scaffold so that the resulting tissue mimics the precise layout of a living organ. A lab-grown pork chop or rack of ribs is perfectly feasible, says Mozdziak. 'When the cultured meat and scaffolding worlds collide, then the industry will take off exponentially,' he says. Lab-grown meat and regenerative organ processes are like looking at the same challenge from two different perspectives. Breakthroughs in one will inevitably lead to breakthroughs in the other.[27] It is interesting to think that the technology we will be using to grow our meats may also bequeath us long and healthy lives. Or we could put it differently. The technology we use to grow our body parts may bequeath us an unlimited supply of meats.

Just a couple of years ago, many futurologists were predicting that lab-grown meats would be in restaurants and stores by about 2030 but the cost of those meats would still be very high. However, the anticipated price of lab-grown meats is falling fast. In March 2017, Memphis Meats told the *Wall Street Journal* that it had gotten the price of a pound of cell-cultured chicken down to USD 9,000. A year later, its CEO announced the price had dropped to below USD 1,000 per pound. In early 2019, the Israeli company, Aleph Farms, told reporters they had gotten a beef patty down to around USD 100 per pound. In April 2019, Bruce Friedrich, the executive director of Good Food Institute, a non-profit organization that supports cell-cultured meat start-ups, estimated a price of 50 dollars. He added that the first meat could just as easily be chicken, fish or something else.[28] Lab-grown meats are species agnostic, in the sense that it does not matter to the technology what meat is grown. It would cost about the same to grow chicken meat, crab meat, foie gras or any other kind of meat with the animals never having been born and never slaughtered. Once whale meat is grown, there would be no reason or excuse for Japan to maintain its whaling ships. Lab-grown meats could be on store shelves as early as 2022 and initially cost a little more than regular meats. With growing production capacities, the price could drop below that of regular meats.

Scaling up the production of lab-grown meat is a little more difficult. One problem is the current lack of suitable equipment. Commercially grown lab-meat will not be in petri dishes but in large vessels called bioreactors. One of the largest bioreactors is with Mosa Meat and is the capacity of 25,000 litres or 25 cubic metres. Post reckons this one reactor could feed 10,000 people. For a cultured meat plant to be commercially viable, it would probably need a series of such or larger capacity bioreactors, which could each be producing different kinds of meats. This problem does not appear to be insurmountable and will happen naturally as demand for cultured meat grows.

A second problem is slightly more intractable. It is regarding the nutrient-rich feedstock on which the cells feed and multiply. Foetal bovine serum (FBS) is an important part of the nutrient-rich solutions, which fuel cell growth in lab-grown meats and other cell culture processes. This is due to it having a very low level of antibodies and containing more growth factors, allowing for versatility in many different cell culture applications. FBS is a byproduct of the dairy industry. It is produced from blood collected at commercial slaughterhouses from dairy cattle that also supply meat intended for human consumption.[29] If lab-grown meats are to replace natural meats and slaughterhouses, the source of FBS will dry up. There are ethical concerns too. Would vegans and vegetarians accept a product that was dependent on slaughterhouses? Understandably, the lab-grown meat industry is scrambling to find alternatives to FBS. A very recent breakthrough may just have made that possible.

That recent breakthrough is a new edible protein product called Solein. Solein has the potential to change our food sources as fundamentally as the first agriculture revolution did 12,000 years ago, when we started depending on agriculture, rather than on hunting and gathering. Just as that agriculture revolution linked food to agriculture, Solein has the potential to delink food from agriculture. Solein contains all the essential amino acids, carbohydrates, fats and vitamins as any other food. Solein is very high in protein—up to 65 per cent. Based on chemical analysis, the essential amino acids also exist in an adequate proportion.[30] It could be an ideal replacement for FBS.

There is no animal or even plant input in the making of Solein. It is quite literally made out of thin air and electricity. The main ingredients of Solein are carbon dioxide, hydrogen, oxygen and nitrogen. Some other nutrients like calcium, phosphorus and potassium are added. These are the same nutrients that plants normally absorb through their roots. Electricity is used for electrolysis of water to release hydrogen. Carbon dioxide, oxygen and nitrogen are captured from the air. Into this nutrient broth containing all the ingredients, specific naturally occurring microbes are introduced, which ingest these ingredients and convert them into Solein. This process is similar to the fermentation that takes place in almost identical fermenters used in breweries or wineries.

Solein is incredibly eco-friendly. It takes 1,550 times as much water to produce the same amount of beef as of Solein and its production is ten times more efficient than that of soy in terms of usable protein yield per acre, even if the land used to generate solar energy needed is taken into account.[31]

Solein was invented by a Finnish tech start-up, Solar Foods. The product was developed in collaboration with VTT Technical Research Centre of Finland and the Lappeenranta-Lahti University of Technology (LUT). The company was formed in November 2017 and started operations in March 2018. The first factory producing Solein is scheduled to open at the end of 2021, producing 50 million meals per year, scaling up to two billion meals by the end of the following year.[32, 33]

Hygiene is another consideration that is likely to induce people towards lab-grown meats. The COVID-19 virus originated from a wet meat market in Wuhan. After Germany thought that it had the virus under control, it flared up again in a meat processing plant in North Rhine-Westphalia in June 2020, infecting over 1,500 people there. There is no chance of viruses transferring from other species to humans through lab-grown meats.

When the Solein plants and the lab-grown meat plants are up and running at speed, in two to five years from now, scientists will have done better than Jesus when he fed a multitude of 5,000 at Bethsaida with two fish and five loaves. Scientists will be feeding billions with just a few cells from a fish or any other animal.

People for the Ethical Treatment of Animals (PETA) supports this development. It has been helping to fund labs and projects involved in cultured meat. While it may at first seem strange for a vegan advocacy organization to support the development of a new type of meat, on reflection, if technology can help end animal suffering in addition to reversing environmental damage, ending world hunger and making our food supply safer, why would PETA not support it? No animal will be caused discomfort. In fact, no animal will be involved at all. Once a few cells are taken from any species and a cell multiplication line started, it could theoretically, go on forever, much like sourdough, dahi or yogurt cultures.

Once cultured meats reach store shelves, how will we react? All meats should cost about the same, as the scarcity of a particular animal or the difficulty in raising it will not matter. Crab and lobster meat will cost about the same as chicken meat. Economics will not matter much in our choice of meat. Societal taboos are a different matter. Considering that any cultured meat we buy from stores, will never have been part of a live animal and no animal will have been either born or slaughtered to put it on the shelves, will our food taboos vanish? Will Hindus be happy to eat a beefsteak? Will Muslims enjoy a rasher of bacon? Will kosher rules have any relevance? Will the biblical injunction, to only have the meat of animals that chew the cud and have cloven hoofs, be ignored? We do not know the answers to these questions and only time can answer them.

What we do know is that we cannot directly ingest proteins from any source. All proteins that we eat are first broken down by our digestive systems into amino acids. There are only twenty amino acids and all meats contain the same amino acids in varying proportions. It is from these amino acids that our bodies construct the hundreds of thousands of proteins that make our bodies work.[34] It is likely that at a later date, we will construct meats that have the right mix of amino acids for different needs, and are not identical to any natural meat at all.

With all the developments in plant and meat production taking place currently and Singapore's reputation for the efficient execution of policies, I am sanguine that Singapore will reach its goal of '30 by 30' well before 2030. By then, it will probably have set a new goal of fifty to sixty by 2040.[34] In December 2020, Singapore became the first country to approve the sale of lab-grown meats.[35]

Let us look at the likely consequences of these developments.

Desirable Consequences:

1. There will be a tremendous increase in the efficiency of farming. Less land and water will be needed for farming.
2. The possibility of global hunger will recede forever if we are able to control population growth.
3. Animal suffering in factory farms and slaughterhouses will come to an end.
4. Vast tracts of land will be freed up from both agriculture and livestock farming.
5. Some of the land freed from agriculture could be allowed to revert back to forest, thereby sequestering some of the excess carbon dioxide and slowing global warming.

Worrisome Consequences:

1. As farming and meat production become automated processes, the worldwide loss of jobs will number in the billions. This will be more so in poorer countries, where a disproportionately large number of livelihoods are dependent on agriculture.
2. Automation will require increasing capital outlays. The small farmer will not be able to compete. The proceeds of agriculture will shift to corporates and shareholders. Inequality will increase.

8

HEALTH AND WELL-BEING

The developments and breakthroughs happening in the medical field are almost too many to enumerate and get a sense of what tomorrow will bring. For this reason, I have broken up the new developments into two parts, the diagnostic and the curative. We first need to diagnose what is wrong with our bodies. It is only then that we can look at what cures are possible.

The lodestar towards which all diagnostic tools are headed is the Tricorder. For those of my readers who have never watched a *Star Trek* serial or movie, let me elaborate. It is a small handheld instrument that can scan just about anything in a human body and come up with any data about the body that is needed. The television series was launched in 1966 and it visualizes space exploration from the mid-twenty-second century to the twenty-fourth century. When the series was launched, the Tricorder was seen as just another science fiction prop in a science fiction series. It had nothing to do with the real world. That perception is now changing. The Tricorder or a device that may mirror it in performance is coming to the real world. The capabilities of the real-world sensing instruments may not match up to the almost miraculous capabilities of the Space Trek Tricorder yet, but it is headed in that direction. It will be here a century or two earlier than what even science fiction writers imagined just fifty years ago.

Until two centuries ago, doctors were pretty much blind to what was happening inside a human body. The stethoscope was invented in 1816. Two centuries later, doctors are seldom seen without a stethoscope draped about their necks. A stethoscope is not much of a diagnostic tool, but it was the only instrument that was accessible to doctors wherever they were. Also, I think a stethoscope became more a statement of the status of the wearer than a diagnostic tool. Fifty years later in 1866, a clinical thermometer, which produced a body temperature in five minutes, was invented. After another thirty years later in 1896, a blood pressure machine, which was then called a tongue-twisting sphygmomanometer, was invented. These, until recently, were the only diagnostic tools readily available to doctors.

There are a number of tests that a doctor today can ask for, but until the test results come in a doctor has only his or her experience to rely upon. The days of a stethoscope as a fashion statement are numbered. It will soon be replaced by a Tricorder-like instrument, which will also be a potent diagnostic tool.

Such a scanning instrument will probably not be called a Tricorder for copyright and other reasons. A possible name for the device may well be Butterfly. That is because the first multipurpose, handheld, ultrasound scanner called Butterfly iQ was launched in 2018 by a Connecticut, US, start-up by the name of Butterfly Network. It has been approved by the Food and Drug Administration of the US for thirteen different conditions, including foetal/obstetrics, muscular-skeletal, ocular areas, cardiovascular and trauma issues. It is more versatile than the large ultrasound machines in hospitals and testing centres and which cost between USD 15,000 and 50,000. It has three transducers but only one probe and can be switched to different modes, such as a Doppler mode to detect blood flow in the peripheral as well as the main blood vessels. It costs under USD 2,000 and can be plugged into a smartphone to watch the scan in real time. It also fits conveniently into a doctor or other healthcare-provider's pocket.

It can also detect cancers. Vascular surgeon John Martin was given a Butterfly iQ to test. He discovered a 3-centimeter mass on his own neck, which turned out to be cancerous.[1] Instruments such as the Butterfly (there are others too like Clarius and Luminify) have a major advantage over other testing methods like X-rays and CT scans. There is no radiation involved, only sound. The radiation emitted by X-rays and CT scans is carcinogenic. The radiation from a CT scan is equivalent to 200 chest X-rays. Researchers estimate that in the US alone, approximately 29,000 cases and 15,000 deaths per year will stem from CT scans alone. The effect of radiation is cumulative and builds up over time and repeated exposure. Children are particularly susceptible to radiation. Other researchers estimate that for every 1,000 children who have an abdominal CT scan, one will develop cancer as a result. A 2012 study that looked at almost 180,000 British children linked CT scans to higher rates of leukaemia and brain cancer.[2] Unfortunately, doctors often have a monetary inducement in ordering CT scans.

Ultrasound devices pose no such hazards and may be freely used. The Butterfly may well become the first interphase between a patient and a doctor. Phrases like 'flitting a Butterfly' over a patient may become standard medical parlance. (As a disclosure, I am not in the pay of Butterfly Network and only know of them from the Internet.)

Apart from ultrasound, other tests too are becoming non-invasive and readily accessible to a doctor. Blood sugar testing has always needed blood, either drawn intravenously or from a finger prick. Diabetics need to, ideally, monitor their blood sugar levels many times a day. This makes the testing both painful and a potential source of infection. Researchers at Massachusetts Institute of Technology (MIT) and the University of Missouri have developed a technique to measure blood sugar levels by shining a laser light on the skin. The study measured the blood glucose levels in twenty healthy non-diabetic adults prior to drinking a glucose-rich beverage. Blood glucose levels were then measured in intervals over the next 160 minutes using three methods: Spectroscopy, IV blood test and finger prick. The results found that spectroscopy predicted values as accurately as a finger-prick test.[3]

Researchers have developed a patch that indicates how much cortisol is being generated through a person's sweat. The hormone cortisol is versatile and influences emotional stress, blood pressure, metabolism, immune response and memory formation. It changes naturally throughout the day and can rise because of increased stress. Contemporary methods for measuring cortisol levels require waiting several days for results from a lab. By the time the results come in, the patient's condition has changed. This is like taking a patient's temperature and learning three days later what the temperature of the patient was three days ago. This is not a very satisfactory state of affairs for a constantly varying level of an important hormone.

In 2018, Alberto Salleo, leading a group of material scientists at Stanford University, created a wearable biosensor which, when applied to the skin, picks up sweat and assesses how much Cortisol a person is producing in seconds, making constant monitoring possible. A paper focused on the wearable sensor was published in *Science Advances*. In the words of Onur Parlak, the lead author of the paper, 'We are particularly interested in sweat sensing, because it offers non-invasive and continuous monitoring of various biomarkers for a range of physiological conditions.' He adds, 'This offers a novel approach for the early detection of various diseases and evaluation of sport performers.' This implies that the group is considering and perhaps working upon the detection of various other biomarkers as well.[4]

Another biomarker is smell. The inspiration to carry out research in this area comes from dogs. For decades, doctors have observed that dogs can detect certain diseases in humans by simply sniffing it out, but scientists still do not understand how dogs are able to spot cancer or diabetes or Parkinson's disease and also tuberculosis and malaria using only their noses. However, advancements over the last few years have brought researchers closer to solving this puzzle, which could lead to revolutionary treatment options for patients with various diseases. It seems that not only do dogs have a vastly greater number of smell receptors in their snouts, their brains are also wired differently. Scientists have already achieved some success in a project sponsored by the Defense Advanced Research Projects Agency (DARPA) of the US department of defense, for the detection of mines and explosives, in a bid to stop using dogs. They are now well on their way to perfecting the technology to detect and even predict various diseases through smells.[5, 6]

There is also evidence that a dog can smell fear and aggression. It is possible that when olfactory science is well understood, it may indicate not only physical diseases but also the frame of mind of a person, becoming an important part of a psychologist's arsenal.

It is a matter of conjecture whether the new non-invasive tests, like blood sugar, cortisol, smell and the others to come, will be added on to an existing platform like the Butterfly iQ, taking it ever closer to the fictional Tricorder in performance, or if they will be stand-alone devices. In either case, a doctor will know far more about a patient within the first fifteen minutes of seeing the patient for the first time than it was ever possible before. Or will a doctor even be involved in the diagnostic process at this point?

Google search is already the bane of doctors. These days when a patient visits a doctor, she has already 'Google searched her symptoms' and has some idea of what the matter with her could possibly be. This puts her in a position to discuss her case with the doctor intelligently or maybe even argue with the doctor. The status of omniscience previously accorded to doctors is fast eroding. A doctor will not be needed for the first evaluation of a patient's condition. A technician will carry out a whole gamut of non-invasive tests and upload the results to a cloud-based AI medical platform. The AI platform will evaluate the test results in a few seconds and forward its assessments to a doctor and the patient along with suggestions for remedial action.

There are many AI-based medical platforms in development that will be able to do such evaluations. In 2015, IBM announced the formation of a special Watson Health division and by mid-2016, Watson Health had acquired four health-data companies for a total cost of about USD 4 billion. It seemed that IBM had the technology, the resources and the commitment necessary to make AI work in healthcare. However, as of now, Watson Health has not been a resounding success.

There are many reasons for this. Watson Health has 15,000 clients and partners. It markets its products to hospitals and individual doctors to help them diagnose and double-check their own diagnoses as well as help insurance companies to settle claims faster. It seems to have left out the most interested party in the health universe—the patient herself. The technology which could, to some extent, have liberated us from doctor and hospital visits, has in effect made us more dependent on them. In an alternative approach, it could design and sell its products to individuals, maintaining each individual's medical history for life. It could start off by storing the full genome sequencing of an individual.

In November 2018, Veritas Genetics, based in Cambridge, Massachusetts, the US, lowered its cost of sequencing a person's entire 6.4 billion base pairs that make up all the DNA coiled up inside our cells, for USD 200, as a promotional exercise. Was Veritas taking a loss on its offer? CEO Mirza Cifric said that it was more than just a holiday season gimmick. 'We're sending a clear signal to the medical research community that the USD 99 genome will be here in three to five years.'[7] To put this in perspective, ninety-nine dollars is about a tenth of what you pay for an iPhone. Why is it important to have your full genome in your medical record? A person's full genome is as intimately a person can be medically known, understood and treated. The genome of a person can indicate the diseases a person is susceptible to, or have a genetic predisposition towards, including different types of cancer, diabetes, heart issues and other ailments. Scientists are constantly discovering sequences in the genome that are linked to different ailments. A good example is when, in 2018, the FDA gave approval to give consumers information about their BRCA1 and BRCA2 genes. More than 1,000 mutations in these genes are known to increase women's chances of breast and ovarian cancers by as much as 75 and 50 per cent respectively. Veritas' tests scan for all of them and, according to the company, turn up five to seven variants of varying concern in those two genes for the average customer.

An AI-based health platform that started with a person's genome and to which the results of all subsequent medical tests and scans was updated, would be impossible to beat as a patient's medical record. With the expertise developed in face recognition technology, it should be possible to train AI to interpret ultrasound images directly. Some other test results will probably need to be entered into the record in a formatted manner to enable the AI in the platform to make a diagnosis. The platform being connected to the web will also take into account any local issues such as any infective diseases being active in any area. If the patient is paying for being on the platform, he or she may choose to share it with a doctor or not, thereby retaining control over one's own life and health. If an insurance company is paying for it, it will likely mandate the compulsory sharing of all data with a doctor.

There will be medico-legal constraints. Doctors' bodies will resist the ability and right of AI platforms to both make a diagnosis and recommend a cure. The AI platform may itself be averse to taking on the responsibility of doing so. To circumvent this, the AI platforms can urge patients to consult a doctor. It could even recommend doctors near to the patient, practising in the relevant field of medicine. If, for example, the patient has an ailment connected to his heart, the names and contact details of cardiologists in the geographical area could be recommended. If, over the period of a decade or so, the AI platform builds up a reputation of being right more often than an average doctor, some patients may prefer to rely on the diagnosis provided by AI. This would depend entirely on two factors. The first is the level of confidence that a particular AI medical platform inspires, largely by its track record. The second is cost. Would it be cheaper to subscribe to an AI platform than to visit a flesh and blood doctor or would it be the other way around? If an AI medical platform can achieve credibility, its clients will not number near the 15,000 clients garnered by Watson Health. They would be counted in millions.

The field of AI-based medical diagnosis is at a nascent stage. As happens in all new fields of endeavour, many start-ups will try out different strategies before some clear trends emerge. Whether or not Watson Health chooses to try a new approach, other companies have entered the fray and some of them are offering their products to individual clients as well.

UK-based start-up Babylon Health is a health subscription-based service that has developed a chatbot for the prevention and diagnosis of disease. Using speech recognition, the chatbot will compare the symptoms that it receives from a user against a database of diseases. In response, it will recommend an appropriate course of action based on a combination of the reported symptoms, patient history and patient circumstances. It has built its database on its 150,000 registered users who currently pay USD 11.40 per month to access Babylon's flagship one-on-one doctor video consultations from a pool of 100 doctors.

Described as a 'personal health companion', Berlin-based Ada Health offers a platform that uses AI and machine learning to track patient health and offers users a better understanding of changes to their health. The platform is offered to individual users, organizations and physicians.[8]

Stanford University researchers have trained an algorithm to diagnose skin cancer using deep learning. The algorithm was trained to detect skin cancer or melanoma using 130,000 images of skin lesions representing over 2,000 different diseases. In the US, there are approximately 5.4 million new skin cancer diagnoses each year and early detection is critical for a greater rate of survival. Early detection correlates with a 97 per cent chance of patients surviving for five years, but drops to 15–20 per cent if detected in Stage-4. A visual examination is the first step of a skin cancer treatment. Stanford's algorithm was tested against twenty-one board-certified dermatologists who reviewed 370 images and were asked if 'they would proceed with a biopsy or reassure the patient' based on each image. Results showed that the algorithm had the same ability as the twenty-one dermatologists in determining the best course of action across all images.[9]

Irrespective of how the technology develops or who pays for it and which companies are the market leaders, there will be one humongous benefit from it. Diagnosis of any sickness will happen much faster than it now does. We have all heard of tragic cases of cancer or other ailments being detected too late for anything to be done about it. This will largely be a thing of the past for those who are enrolled onto an AI health program. Early detection of a disease is winning more than half the battle against it. This, by itself, will result in fewer deaths and hence, longer life expectancies.

Let us now move on from the diagnostic part of developing healthcare to the curative part of it. Many of the new developments are arising from interplays between AI and microbiology, including the genome analysis of both patients and pathogens. These are areas that will lead to the quick development of vaccines as well as speeding up the development of new, better-targeted antibiotics. New drug creation too will be revolutionized. 3D printing will make individually designed prosthetic limbs possible. Bio-printers will be able to fabricate body parts from the cells of the patients themselves. Robotic surgery, which is routine for cataracts and inserting corneas in eyes, will cover an increasing range of body parts. While work is going on in these and more areas, much of that work has started in earnest only in the past five years or so. It may well be another five to ten years for it all to come to fruition.

As I write this in April 2020, we are in the midst of the

Coronavirus or SARS-CoV-19 pandemic. Coffins are being counted with morbid curiosity and panic engulfs many parts of the globe. There is a sense of helplessness prevailing the world over. Most of us, however, may be missing to notice the rapidity with which vaccines for the virus have been developed.

Vaccination began in 1796 when Edward Jenner, an English physician, noticed that people who had been infected with cowpox, a very mild illness, did not contract smallpox, a serious and at times, a fatal illness. He purposefully infected a thirteen-year-old boy with cowpox, preventing the boy from contracting smallpox and thereby, proving the effectiveness of vaccination. This led to many other vaccines being created with Louis Pasteur developing vaccines for cholera and anthrax. Vaccines for other diseases followed.

The theory is straightforward. Viruses are isolated from patients and then either weakened with chemicals or killed outright. The weakened virus or the remnants of the dead virus is injected into people who have to be vaccinated against a particular disease. The recipients of the vaccine suffer a minor illness in the case of the weakened virus and are not made ill at all in the case of the dead virus. However, the body's immune system recognizes the inactivated virus as an intruder and prepares antibodies against it. When an actual virus threatens, defences against it are in place. These processes are time-consuming and involve many trials and errors. They are also difficult to scale up because of the quantity of the virus, which has to be first collected and deactivated.

A vaccine, in other words, works by training the immune system. Even a dead virus can train the immune system because of molecules called antigens, which are present on all viruses and bacteria and are a sort of a marker for the pathogen. By injecting these antigens into the body, the immune system can safely learn to recognize them as hostile invaders, produce antibodies and remember them for the future. If the antigen reappears in a fresh infection, the immune system will recognize it and attack aggressively before the pathogen can cause sickness.

The new breakthrough in vaccine development has come after we learnt to easily read the genome of any organism. Vaccines made in this new way are also referred to as DNA vaccines and are still in the experimental stage. They dispense with all the unnecessary parts of the virus or bacterium and instead contain just an injection of a few parts of the pathogen's DNA. These DNA strands would instruct the body's own cells to make the antigens of the virus. The immune system will recognize the antigens as intruders and start making antibodies to fight the virus. As a result, these vaccines would be very efficient immune system trainers. They are also cheap and easy to produce in large quantities.[10]

To get an idea about the speed with which vaccines can be developed, it is interesting to follow the timeline of development of the COVID-19 vaccine by Moderna Therapeutics, a Massachusetts, US-based company. On January 11 2020, Chinese authorities shared the genetic sequence of the novel coronavirus. On 13 January, that is, in just two days, the US National Institutes of Health and Moderna's infectious disease research team finalized the sequence for mRNA-1273, the company's vaccine against the virus. On 7 February, the first clinical batch, including fill and finishing of vials, was completed, that is, in just twenty-five days, from sequence selection to vaccine manufacture. The expected delay of twelve to eighteen months before the vaccine is ready to be given to the public at large is because of trials and safety protocols. In view of the cascading infections worldwide, this period is likely to be reduced. Moderna, meanwhile, is scaling up its ability to make millions of doses per month.[11] In early November 2020 Pfizer, a major pharmaceutical company, said it had developed a vaccine against the virus, which was more than 90 per cent effective. A few days later Moderna made a similar statement.

There is yet more developmental work being done on new vaccine platforms. Research is moving from DNA vaccines to synthetic biology or synbio vaccines. A vaccine created through the tinkering of synbio looks not only scalable to a level of billions but will also work without refrigerating, an important quality for some parts of the world. Synbio vaccines contain synthetic (that is lab-made) strands of DNA or RNA that code for protein molecules on the virus's surface. Once the vaccine delivers the genetic material to the body's cells, the cells make the antigens to prime the immune system. A vaccine can be studded with the genetic material of more than one virus, making it possible to have a vaccine that is effective against multiple viruses.

Researchers are cautiously optimistic because of a recent success. An experimental vaccine against respiratory syncytial virus (RSV), the main cause of pneumonia in children, is also made of a computer-designed nanoparticle that self-assembles from proteins and is studded with an engineered version of RSV's key antigen. When tested in mice and monkeys, it produced ten times more antibodies than vaccines made traditionally.[12]

With the major breakthroughs happening in vaccines, it is likely that the currently ravaging COVID-19 may well turn out to be the last pandemic to torment humanity. Any new virus that comes our way will generate an almost instant reaction from vaccine makers, and the infection will be nipped in the bud well before it becomes the sole topic of discussion in newspapers and talk shows. It is a tantalizing thought that if COVID-19 had happened a few years later, it would never have reached the stage of becoming a pandemic.

While there are some anti-viral drugs, our chief weapon against viruses is vaccination. Our chief weapon against bacterial infections are antibiotics. Penicillin was the first antibiotic that was discovered. It was discovered in 1928 and started being used as an anti-bacterial in 1942. Thereafter, many more antibiotics have been discovered. Antibiotics ushered in a new age of medicine. No doctor practising today can imagine medicine without antibiotics. The reason we can safely use antibiotics is that we, along with all other animals and plants, belong to the domain of life known as eukaryotes. The cells that make up our bodies have a nucleus enclosed within cell walls or membranes. The other two domains of life, bacteria and archaea, are prokaryotes and have no cell wall protected organelles. When we take antibiotics, the cells that make up our bodies are not affected, whereas the bacteria in our bodies can be killed.

While being a major weapon against disease, there are two problems with antibiotics. The first is that antibiotics are largely indiscriminate in killing bacteria. Not all bacteria in or on our bodies are pathogens. With many, we have evolved into a symbiotic relationship and they help us in ways not completely yet understood. The second is that with the continuous use of antibiotics, many strains of bacteria have acquired immunity against antibiotics. We normally take for granted that any infectious disease is curable by antibiotic therapy. Antibiotics are manufactured at an estimated scale of about 100,000 tons annually worldwide. Many pathogens have become resistant to multiple antibiotics, and we have the phenomenon of multidrug resistance. Indeed, some strains have become resistant to practically all of the commonly available agents. A notorious case is the Methicillin-resistant Staphylococcus Aureus (MRSA), which is resistant to almost every antibiotic and is a major source of hospital-acquired infections.[13] The situation is so alarming that some fear we may be regressing medically to the time before antibiotics.

Fortunately, there are glimmerings of hope that we may not be left without any protection against microbes. The hope comes from new ways to harness Clustered Regularly Interspaced Short Palindromic Repeat (CRISPR) as a tool against bacteria. CRISPR is a powerful and precise tool for gene editing that allows scientists to target and activate or silence individual genes. It allows researchers to easily alter DNA sequences and modify gene function. Its many potential applications include correcting genetic defects, treating and improving crops and so on. It has been considered for altering mosquitoes so they cannot spread malaria and editing tomatoes, so they are more flavourful. Now researchers are harnessing

CRISPR to turn a bacterium's machinery against itself or against viruses that infect human cells. But what exactly is CRISPR and what else can it do?

CRISPR is an acronym that stands for 'Clustered Regularly Interspaced Short Palindromic Repeats'. This expansion of the acronym is something that will make no sense to you unless you happen to be a professional geneticist. To try and understand it, we need to go back to Biology 101. Every living thing we see around us with our naked eyes is a eukaryote and that includes us and all the other animals and all plants. We evolved around two billion years ago, give or take a couple of hundred million years. Bacteria and archaea are prokaryotes, which we need a microscope to see and were here long before us. The first microbes evolved around three and a half billion years ago when the newly formed earth was still very young. We did not invent CRISPR, the prokaryotes did. They beat us to it by well over two billion years. It turns out that CRISPR is the immune system of bacteria and archaea against viruses. We just understood it a few years back.

In bacterial DNA, the CRISPR sequences are the DNA records of previous infections. If a new infection corresponds to previously existing sequences, it triggers a response to attack the new infection. In CRISPR technology, the protein Cas9 (or CRISPR associated) is an enzyme that acts as a pair of molecular scissors capable of cutting strands of DNA at any precise point and thereby editing genes as required.[14] What scientists are endeavouring to do is to turn the immune system of the bacteria against itself.

'CRISPR is the next step in antimicrobial therapy,' said David Edgell, a biologist at the Western University in London, Ontario and lead author of a study published in October 2019. In their recent study, Dr Edgell and his colleagues successfully used a CRISPR-associated enzyme called Cas9 to eliminate a species of salmonella by inducing it to make lethal cuts to its own genome. The team began with a conjugated plasmid, a small packet of genetic material that can replicate itself and be passed from one bacterium to the next. To the plasmid, the scientists added the coded instructions for CRISPR enzymes that would target salmonella DNA. The plasmid was then tucked inside *E. coli* bacteria. The *E. coli* could then transfer the engineered plasmid to the salmonella, where the CRISPR system would activate, destroying the bacteria. That is exactly what the researchers observed in a petri dish. The CRISPR system wiped out nearly all salmonella bacteria, while leaving *E. coli* intact.[15]

It is early days still for this technology, but it is for the first time that doctors, who had been gloomily eyeing their existing arsenal of antibiotics of dwindling effectiveness, feel a ray of hope. Not only can they hope to have a potent weapon against microbes again, but that weapon can be accurately targeted at specific microbes, eliminating collateral damage to friendly bacteria.

Some types of cancer, such as cervical and liver cancers, are caused by viruses (oncoviruses). Traditional vaccines against those viruses, such as the HPV vaccine and the hepatitis B vaccine, prevent those types of cancer. Other cancers are to some extent caused by bacterial infections (for example, stomach cancer and *Helicobacter pylori*).[16] With the recent breakthroughs in vaccine development, we can expect to see some breakthroughs in cancer vaccines.

We may, in the years to come, look back on the coronavirus pandemic as the single incident that gave a strong impetus to put the rapid development of both vaccines and antibiotics on the fast track. The old adage of necessity being the mother of invention seems to be at work here. Testing protocols and periods too will be speeded up irreversibly without adverse consequences.

Another area of research is the growing of human organs in petri dishes or even being printed out by 3D bioprinters. While there are many hurdles to overcome before you can go and grow yourself a new heart, the technology is not completely out of reach. To get an idea of where we are on the road map to a new heart, liver or limb, consider what has already been achieved.

Researchers at Massachusetts General Hospital grew an entire rat arm in a dish. The bioengineered rat forelimb contained bone, cartilage, blood vessels, tendons, ligaments and nerves and could pave the way for entire limb transplants for amputees. Scientists from the Institute of Molecular Biotechnology in Vienna, Austria, announced they had successfully created a mini brain in the lab. Using stem cells, they grew a model of a developing brain that was about the size of an embryonic human brain at nine weeks old. It did not look like a brain, but it had active neurons and had much the same organizational structure.[17]

In June 2019, a team of Japanese researchers developed a mini brain that shows not only the complex three-dimensional structure of the cerebral cortex, but also coordinated neural activity. The brain is a jarring example of how good scientists are getting at rebuilding organs from scratch. The artificial neurons behave like those in our brain.[18] By the time a foetus is six months old, it is producing electrical signals recognizable as brain waves. Clusters of lab-grown brain cells, known as organoids, seem to follow a similar schedule. 'After these organoids are in the six-to-nine month range, that's when (the electrical patterns) start to look a lot like what you'd see with a preterm infant,' says Alysson Muotri, director of the Stem Cell Program at the University of California, San Diego.[19]

Any breakthroughs made in the science of growing organs in petri dishes will also be useful for those trying to grow meats in petri dishes. Some of the breakthroughs made by the meat-growing industry may be useful to the scientists trying to grow organs. The two endeavours could leapfrog over each other as they rush towards their separate goals.

Work is also ongoing to 3D print body parts in a process called bioprinting. Bioprinting originated in the early 2000s, when it was discovered that living cells could be sprayed through the nozzles of inkjet printers without being damaged. Today, using multiple printing heads to squirt out different cell types, along with polymers that help the structure keep its shape, it is possible to deposit layer upon layer of cells that will bind together and grow into living, functional tissue. Researchers are tinkering with kidney and liver tissues, skin, bones and cartilage, as well as the networks of blood vessels needed to keep body parts alive. They have implanted printed ears, and also muscles, into animals and watched these integrate properly with their hosts. In 2016, a group at Northwestern University even printed working bio-prosthetic ovaries for mice. The recipients were able to conceive and give birth with the aid of these artificial organs.[20]

Robotic surgeries have almost become routine. Intuitive Surgical Inc. is an American corporation that develops, manufactures and markets robotic products designed to improve clinical outcomes of patients through minimally invasive surgery, most notably with its da Vinci Surgical system. As of 31 December 2019, it had an installed base of 5,582 da Vinci Surgical Systems all over the world. It is the leader in the industry and in 2019, its systems performed over one and a quarter million surgical procedures.

But what exactly do we mean by the term 'robotic surgery'? It is a procedure where the surgeon does not hold a scalpel and sutures in his or her hands but sits on a control panel and controls the instruments which perform the surgery more finely than human hands could, limiting the size of the incision, and ensuring faster healing rates. It is a big improvement on traditional surgical procedures, where surgeons needed to make large incisions to get at the affected area.[21] But is it really robotic surgery or simply a human surgeon using better surgical instruments? There is no automation or AI involved.

That may be changing. TransEnterix Inc. is another company that provides robotic surgery systems. In March 2020, the company received something called 510 (k), clearance from the FDA for the Intelligent Surgical Unit that enables machine vision capabilities on their Senhance Surgical System. 'We are pleased to have received this important clearance earlier than expected.

Machine vision is the next major advance in digital surgery,' said Anthony Fernando, TransEnterix president and CEO. 'Our system is designed to significantly advance the sensing capabilities of computer-assisted surgery. With this hardware and software system, the Senhance System will gather and interpret visual information from the surgical field. The capabilities now cleared will be focused on optimizing visualization and camera control in ways never before offered in robotic or digital surgery. These initial capabilities represent the first step in our journey to bring the benefits of augmented intelligence and machine vision to surgery.'[21] What this implies is that AI is stepping into surgery. As this capability progresses, the involvement of the surgeon will progressively reduce. The day will come when the surgeon will monitor the ongoing surgery on his or her console, with perhaps a hand on the manual override button in case something unexpected happens.

'Prosthetics and implants' is another area in which we can expect further developments. Medical implants and devices are already being widely used today. They range from tooth implants to knee and hip and shoulder joint replacements, to prosthetic limbs and pacemakers, to ventricular assist devices, spinal cord stimulators (chronic pain management), deep brain stimulators (to control symptoms of conditions such as Parkinson's disease, essential tremor, epilepsy and depression), cochlear implants (enabling hearing) and more recently, bionic eyes (restore vision) are a large and rapidly growing sector of the medical device market.[23]

Research on implants and prosthetics is ongoing at a frenetic pace all over the world. It would need a hefty tome to do any kind of justice to the volume of ongoing work. It is impossible to even allude to all of it in a couple of paragraphs. I will mention two aspects of pathbreaking research to give a flavour of the ongoing research.

Painful knees are a bane of an aging population. A team of

scientists may have finally found a way to replace knee cartilage after injuries or normal wear and tear of aging. Cartilage cannot be grown back but a hydrogel that is both strong and flexible enough to survive the abuse while cushioning knees has been developed at Duke University, *Science Alerts* reported in June 2020. Duke University chemist, Ben Wiley says simply, 'We set out to make the first hydrogel that has the properties of cartilage.' If the material gets approved for clinical use, it could present an alternative to far more invasive and often short-lived knee replacement surgeries. In tests, it has been squished by 100-pound weights, yanked and stretched 100,000 times and been rubbed against natural cartilage a million times. The team expects it would take at least three years to get regulatory approval.[23]

Researchers at the University of Chicago are leading a project to introduce a sense of touch to the latest brain-controlled prosthetic limbs. Adding sensory feedback to already complex neuroprosthetics is a towering task but offers the chance to radically transform the lives of amputees and people with paralysis. As University of Chicago associate professor and neuroprosthetics researcher Dr Sliman Bensmaia says, 'The idea is to put electrodes in the motor cortex, so when a tetraplegic patient tries to move their arm, or imagines moving their arm, there is a characteristic pattern of activation in this motor part of the brain.' He adds, 'We can take the signals from this part of the brain, and infer what the patient or subject wanted to do, and then you make the robotic arm do that.'

One of the major limiting factors for the dexterity of neuroprosthetics relates to a sense of touch, which humans take for granted. Bensmaia, along with others, is working to advance the understanding and implementation of that on the system that transmits sensory information from the body's nerve fibres to the brain's somatosensory cortex, making the bionic limb act and feel as if it were your own.[24]

Bionic Woman or Bionic Man may not be an impossible fantasy after all.

Another area of human health and well-being that researchers have started looking at seriously is human life extension. Long and eternal life has always fascinated mankind. In one of the oldest stories of mankind, *The Epic of Gilgamesh*, written in Sumerian about 4,200 ago, the hero Gilgamesh, king of Uruk, sets out to undertake a long and perilous journey to discover the secret of eternal life. The patriarchs of the Old Testament were ascribed ages of hundreds of years with Methuselah living to be 969 years of age. More recently, Juan Ponce de León, a Spanish conquistador, went in search of a rumoured fountain of youth at the start of the sixteenth century.

Outside of legends, human life expectancy has increased dramatically over the last two hundred years. It has increased worldwide from twenty-seven years in 1800 to seventy-two years in 2015. For some countries, it has been even more dramatic over the last century. A century ago, life expectancy in India and South Korea was twenty-three years. A century later, life expectancy in India has almost tripled and in South Korea, it has almost quadrupled.[26]

This increase in life expectancy has been achieved largely due to a few reasons, such as reduced child mortality, better health care and hygiene, healthier lifestyles, sufficient food and improved medical care. This increase has not been because of any research on aging per se. This is now changing. Serious research is now being conducted on two aspects of growing old. The first is about extending our lifespans or adding years to life. An informal target age is the one attained by Frenchwoman Jeanne Calment, who had the longest verified lifespan of 122 years, 164 days. The second is about reducing senescence or the effects of old age such as dementia, diminishing memory, cognition, sight, hearing, taste and communication as well as other diseases associated with old age. This is about adding life to years. It is too early to speculate where this ongoing research will take us, but I think it is safe to assume that children being born today in some parts of the world can expect to live healthy productive lives of well over a hundred years.[27, 28]

A whole new world of medicine and healthcare awaits us. It will be very different from the way medicine was practised in the twentieth century and much of it will be in place by the end of the 2020s. Let us see what the consequences of the coming changes will be.

Desirable Consequences:

1. Early detection and rapid cure of most diseases will ensure healthier lives.
2. People will live longer with the number of centenarians increasing dramatically.
3. While generally healthier than older people today, old age will still have its own limitations. The demand for more nurses and other caregivers, including physiotherapists, will grow exponentially.
4. With machines and AI performing much of the diagnostic and curative procedures, the need for more lab and machine technicians will grow.
5. As new advances are made in the medical field, researchers, both doctors and people in other sciences, will find new avenues of work opening up for them.

Worrisome Consequences:

1. Doctors with small medical practices will either be squeezed out or the practices will be manned by technicians, who will conduct the basic tests, and upload the data to an AI-based system. If needed, the data may then be reviewed by specialists before a cure is prescribed.
2. Individual medical practices will become medical data collection centres of large health corporations, manned by technicians. Doctors with once thriving practices will be marginalized, becoming at best, salaried employees.

PART TWO

JOB CREATION

9

CONSEQUENCES AND COCKAIGNE

The changes heading our way that I have mentioned so far, are certainly not comprehensive. There are many other areas with equally fascinating breakthroughs. Indeed, it is difficult to think of an area that has not experienced change. Invariably, the change is towards greater efficiencies, better products at lower costs. For me, the most astounding takeaway is that the breakthroughs are all happening more or less simultaneously. It is as if we have reached a certain preordained age like children. All children stand up and take their first steps when they are a year old. Some may do so a little earlier and some a little later but that is when children start walking. It seems that all fields of endeavour have now reached the walking age.

I could keep writing about more industries, but this book would never finish then. However, I will, very briefly, touch upon three areas of activity that cater to basic human needs. In India, we refer to them as *'Roti, Kapda aur Makan'*. That translates to the three basic needs—food for the belly, clothes on our backs and a roof over our heads. Providing for each one of these three basic needs gives employment to untold millions.

We have already seen the developments happening in farming and the growing of meats. The step between the growing of foods and eating them is processing and cooking them. This, until recently, involved human labour, whether in the form of salaried jobs or cooking food at home. The picture is fast changing. Industrially manufactured foods such as ketchup or frozen pizza or baby food or anything that you buy pre-packed and more or less ready to eat, with perhaps a little heating, is manufactured in increasingly automated plants. Restaurants, specially fast-food restaurants, are rapidly embracing AI and automation. The critical requirements of fast-food restaurants are the uniformity of products, economics and speed. All three requirements are best served with automation. Greg Creed, CEO of Yum Brands, which owns several fast-food restaurant chains, including Pizza Hut, KFC and Taco Bell, stated the belief that fast-food robots, automation and AI, could replace humans in fast-food establishments by the middle of the 2020s.[1]

There are an estimated 4 million employees working in the fast-food industry and about 10 million in other restaurants in the US.[2] I can only estimate the worldwide employment of fast-food workers at about 25 million and the other restaurant workers at about 150 million. In any case, the restaurant industry is a major employment source. While it is too early to even hazard a guess about the jobs that will be lost to automation in eateries, we can safely say it will be in the millions.

Far more cooking is done in homes than in restaurants in most parts of the world. The time spent in cooking does not show up in any employment figures but that does not alter the fact that billions of man hours or woman hours are spent in the kitchen. If many of these man or woman hours were freed up, I have no idea how they might be spent. There are probably as many answers as there are people. Unless your passion is cooking, it is normally regarded as an unavoidable chore. If automation and AI were to take over your chore, you would be the master of the hours freed up. Cooking automation for homes has arrived. Many companies the world over are working to perfect cooking machines for different cuisines. Vorwerk is a German company and their cooking machine Thermomix is one of the leading cooking machines sold across the world. Their latest model, Thermomix TM6, comes with an astonishing twenty functions, including whisking, caramelizing, steaming, emulsifying and grinding. It can be connected to a Wi-Fi to download thousands of recipes. A freshly cooked meal, starting with basic ingredients, can be made in half an hour.[3] A few Indian start-ups are in the process of developing robotic cooking machines with a focus on different Indian cuisines, as are companies in East Asia, focusing on their cuisines. Many of these machines can be preloaded with the needed ingredients and a signal can be sent to them when a person leaves the office, so that a hot meal is ready on reaching home. It is a matter of a few years for viable alternatives to ordering home-delivered meals will be readily available in the form of automatically cooked food in each kitchen, which will be both healthier and cheaper. The coronavirus pandemic will exacerbate health and safety concerns, putting the multibillion-dollar food delivery industry under pressure. Millions of jobs in the industry will be lost to robots in every kitchen.

Now, consider the clothes on your back. If you have recently bought a shirt or other article of clothing, anywhere in the world, there are good chances that it was made in Bangladesh or Sri Lanka or one of a few other countries that make clothes for the world. This is set to change. Automated garment-making is already here. Low-priced garments are only possible because of low production cost. Earlier, this had been possible by having them manufactured in low-cost countries with relatively lower paid workers. Now garments will be made by machines, which are not paid at all.

Work on automated sewing began at Georgia Tech's Advanced Technology Development Center more than a decade ago. Strangely, the research was given a push by DARPA, the advanced research projects wing of the US department of defense. This was because US law mandated that uniforms for defence personnel only be procured from American manufacturers. As a result, we now have automated sewing machines, unsurprisingly called Sewbots. One such Sewbot known as LOWRY, from SoftWear Automation, can now sew more accurately and faster than humans. Fabric is a difficult material to work with. It is flexible, and it stretches, warps and folds. It takes years to train a human to become good at it. LOWRY, with its special camera, can follow individual threads in the fabric, one thousand times a second, giving its stitching an accuracy impossible for humans to match.

A robotic sewing production line needs about 70 per cent less humans to run it and is about 70 per cent faster too. Using robotics makes the cost of producing a shirt in the US comparable to one produced overseas. For example, in Bangladesh the labour cost to produce a denim shirt is about USD 0.22. If made by US workers, that labour cost jumps to USD 7.47, but with a robotic production line, it is just USD 0.33 per shirt.[4] In the case of America and Bangladesh, the US produces large amounts of cotton and Bangladesh none at all. The cotton or the cloth made with it has to first be shipped halfway around the world and the finished goods then shipped all the way back.

Millions of workers, mostly in Asia, employed in making garments, will find in a few years that the companies they work for have no further production orders.

Let us now consider the roofs over our heads. The construction industry, which builds living spaces for us, along with our offices, shopping malls, and just about any kind of structure, employs millions of people in every sizable country. Will jobs be lost here also? I will give two recent developments in construction and let the reader draw her own inferences.

House construction has not changed much over the last century. The last major breakthrough was steel-reinforced concrete slabs for the roof of each level. A major component of the cost of a house is the labour cost. House building is also time-consuming. There are two developments, which are changing the picture completely. One is the 3D printing of houses and the other is prefabricated construction. The two approaches to house building can be linked together, when the prefabricated parts of a building are 3D printed with all the precision needed to put the parts together.

ICON, a company in Austin, Texas, USA, specializes in developing low-cost construction solutions. Their highlight project is 3D printing a 650-square-foot sturdy house, complete with doors and windows, for USD 4,000 in twenty-four hours. That is possibly less time than it took the builders of my granddaughter's dollhouse to make it. In collaboration with non-profit organization New Story, ICON plans to build a whole neighbourhood of these low-cost 3D printed houses in El Salvador. The goal is to provide homes for people who do not as yet have one.[5, 6]

In 2015, Broad Sustainable Building, a prefab Chinese construction company put up a fifty-seven-floor skyscraper in nineteen days, assembling three floors a day using a modular method. The building is large. It has nineteen atriums, 800 apartments and office space for 4,000 people. The structure is safe and can withstand earthquakes according to Xiao Changgeng, the vice president of the company. The company now has ambitions to assemble the world's tallest skyscraper at 220 floors, in only three months.[7]

It is clear that the construction industry is set for major changes. The construction of individual houses and large buildings will become both cheaper and quicker but will need fewer workers. The loss of jobs in the construction industry will be in millions. However, seeing the speed with which tall large structures can now be built, I am now more optimistic about Professor Eric Loth's wind turbines of 50 MWs each and also about Professor Dickson Despommier's thirty-storey vertical farms, each able to feed 50,000 people.

No matter what sphere of human activity we look at, the trends all point in the same direction. Better goods, more goods, cheaper goods, longer, healthier lives but fewer jobs. It is not only physical goods but many services too. The best education can reach anywhere on the planet (in my earlier book, *The Economic Reactor*,[8] I had shared my views on education). Pursuits that were once expensive, like music and photography, are now virtually free.

There are two prisms we can view this situation through. One is a prism through which we look despairingly at the vast majority of us being formally unemployed and the other is the prism through which we rejoice at the plentitude of things available to us. Both views are pertinent to our lives. Let us first look through the prism of joyous plentitude. For the time being, please put away your concerns about the job situation, money and economics as a whole. We will come back to that soon enough.

For the first time in human history, automated intelligent machines and AI will be able to meet almost all our needs. Most of us will not need to work, that being the corollary to fewer jobs being available. The few of us who work with the machines we have invented, will be able to provide us all with the food we could desire, the clothes we want and nice dwelling places, all the while ensuring long and healthy lives for us and providing us with entertainment and education if we so desire. This is nothing but a description of Cockaigne.

Cockaigne was a medieval European myth. It was a veritable land of milk and honey, even though imaginary. It was even given an approximate location as being somewhere west of Spain. There were slightly differing versions of Cockaigne in different European countries, but the descriptions tallied. Amongst the better known sources of what Cockaigne was like was a thirteenth-century French poem called, 'The Land of Cockaigne', which has been translated into modern English.[9] It depicts that everything is there for the taking, food perfectly cooked, all imaginable meats and wine. The poem is quite libidinous and talks of monks and nuns frolicking sexually. Another source is an oil painting, 'The Land of Cockaigne' by Pieter Bruegel in 1567, which shows people redolent with food sprawled supine. According to Herman Pleij, professor emeritus of medieval Dutch literature at the University of Amsterdam,

> 'Roasted pigs wander about with knives in their backs to make carving easy, where grilled geese fly directly into one's mouth,

> where cooked fish jump out of the water and land at one's feet. The weather is always mild, the wine flows freely, sex is readily available, and all people enjoy eternal youth.'[10]

Roasted pigs with knives in their backs and grilled geese flying directly into one's mouth may not be to everyone's taste, but there is no mistaking the sense of overwhelming abundance of all things pleasurable in Cockaigne. The world we are creating will also give us abundance, but there is one very important difference. Cockaigne was a pleasurable fantasy. Nobody really expected to live there or even see it. There was no reason to worry about any consequences that might arise from such living. We do not have that luxury. We need to be aware of the world we are stepping into, its pitfalls and its opportunities.

Our species has never experienced as much abundance as we are now capable of generating with very few of us contributing to that abundance. It will be a new experience for us. It will change us in many ways. It will change our social structure and it will change our economic system. It may also change us as a species. This last change will not be immediate, but there are some straws in the wind, which indicate that change we will.

We, as a species, consider ourselves to be a brainy one, which we are if we compare the mass of our brain with the rest of our body mass. It is far greater than what other species have. Our brain is our chief tool of survival and it is because of our brains that we have acquired supremacy over other life forms on the earth and the ability to alter our planet. This is not a value statement but merely a statement of fact. We also tend to believe that we are brainier than our earliest ancestors, the Cro-Magnons from who we are descended and who were in Europe 20,000 to 30,000 years ago, or our Stone Age ancestors. This last, however, is not true.

As we started evolving from the primates, through the various hominid species to the Cro-Magnons (who are now referred to as EEMH or European Early Modern Humans), the size of our brain kept increasing. Then surprisingly, about 10,000 years ago, sizes of the human brain started reducing. Cro-Magnons had the largest brains of all human species. Our brains are now smaller. Male brains have shrunk by about 10 per cent and female brains by about 17 per cent.[11]

The brain is a very expensive organ to maintain. The human brain weighs about 2 per cent of our body weight but uses about 25 per cent of the blood flow and energy consumed by the whole body. Evolution will not permit the unnecessary growth of such an expensive organ. We can only surmise that with the much harsher conditions that the Cro-Magnons were living in, they needed more intelligence to survive and reproduce. The struggle to eat and not be eaten, to find a mate and raise children to maturity needed much more savvy than it now does. David Geary, a curators' distinguished professor with interests in mathematical cognition and learning as well as the biological bases of sex differences, argues that as human society gets more complex, individuals do not need to be as intelligent to survive. It is as if we have built an exoskeleton for our brains, comprising of folklore, the dos and don'ts of religion, and accepted wisdom, books and now the Internet. We do not have to think through every mundane situation from scratch. Also, the time of 10,000 years ago, when our brains started shrinking, dovetails nicely with the start of the agricultural revolution and civilization, providing an easier existence to us. [12]

Now that we are approaching a time when our machines will provide us with our needs, it would be reasonable to expect that our brains will shrink even faster. How much faster is a matter of conjecture. One laboratory experiment, however, points to a rapid decline of our abilities when everything needed for our sustenance is readily available.

In the 1960s, Sol Spiegelman, a molecular biologist, conducted an experiment on RNA molecules of a simple bacteriophage which literally means, 'bacteria eater'. The experiment consisted of a series of test tubes into which he put an RNA replication enzyme, some free nucleotides and some salts or in other words all the nutrition that the RNA would need to eat and multiply. He added the RNA molecules into the first test tube. The molecules multiplied. After some time, he took a few drops from the first test tube and put them into the second test tube. Again, after some time, he took a few drops from the second test tube and put them in the third tube and so on until the seventy-fourth test tube. Maybe he then ran out of test tubes. Each shift of a few drops into the next test tube represented a generational change. The last test tube told the story of what would happen after seventy-four generations of freely feeding a strain of RNA molecules without them having to do anything. At the start of the experiment, the strand of RNA molecules comprised 4,500 nucleotide bases. After seventy-four generations of easy living, the molecule was reduced to 218 nucleotides and came to be called Spiegelman's Monster. A repeat of this experiment in 1997 showed that the Spiegelman Monster eventually becomes even shorter, containing only forty-eight or fifty-four nucleotides. That is just about 1 per cent of the original RNA strand.[13]

What happens to an RNA molecule, under certain conditions, cannot be extrapolated to what would happen to larger organisms and certainly not to human beings. The only relevant inference we can draw from this experiment is that evolution is not wasteful of resources. As long as an organism can sustain itself and multiply, evolution will readily surrender any other attributes the organism may have.

The domestication of wild animals is another straw in the wind that points in the same direction. The sustained selection for lower reactivity among domesticated animals has resulted in profound changes in brain form and function. The larger was the size of the brain to begin with, and the greater its degree of folding, the greater was the degree of brain size reduction under domestication. Foxes that had been selectively bred for tameness over forty years only had experienced a significant reduction in brain size, which supports the hypothesis that brain size reduction is an early response to domestication. The most affected portion of the brain in domestic animals is the limbic system, which in domestic dogs, pigs, and sheep show a 40 per cent reduction in size compared with their wild species. This portion of the brain regulates endocrine function that influences behaviours such as aggression, wariness, and responses to stress.[14]

Again, what happens to domesticated animals cannot be extrapolated to what happens to humans. However, it is interesting to note that in domesticated animals, the limbic system and thereby, endocrine functioning is the most and speedily affected area of the brain. It is the endocrine, which directly affects the production of testosterone and of spermatozoa.[15] Both testosterone levels and sperm counts have been falling worldwide since about the 1960s. Various reasons have been put forward, including pollution and job stresses, but none of the reasons has withstood scrutiny. Testing for both levels has been done in the more advanced economies and the better-off sections of men in other countries. The 1960s onwards has marked an era of rising prosperity and the emergence of a welfare state, in what is loosely referred to as the western world. Have rising prosperity and the comforts of a welfare state domesticated us? Could we conclude that what we are seeing simply is what is seen in all domesticated animals? Will our machines, which will provide us with everything, domesticate us further?

Shrinking brains, Spiegelman Monsters and dropping sperm counts are possibly nothing more than my musings and of no immediate concern. Let us now turn to matters of more immediate concern, which are jobs, money and the economy.

There is another big difference between Cockaigne and our coming world. In Cockaigne, there was an abundance of all goods of high quality and they were free for the taking. In our coming world too, there will be an abundance of goods of high quality, but they will not be free for the taking. The goods that AI and our machines provide us may be relatively cheap, but they will have to be paid for. In a world largely without jobs, how will we be able to pay for the goods? The obvious solution is to give everyone some money to pay for them.

I am aware that the last sentence has probably alienated a large number of readers. I can understand their alienation. When I first came across the idea of a Universal Basic Income (UBI) that was my reaction also. Simply giving money to people would turn them into parasites on society, living off the labours of those who work. After mulling over the coming paucity of jobs for over a year, I realized that the problem could be solved by altering the concept of a UBI to that of a Universal Supplementary Income or USI. Not only could the problem of no money be solved, USI could, under the right conditions, become a very powerful engine of economic growth. Please bear with me until the next chapter.

10

UNIVERSAL SUPPLEMENTARY INCOME

The difference between a Universal Basic Income (UBI) and a Universal Supplementary Income (USI) is just what the terms say. A UBI is money handed out by the government to meet the basic expenses of a person, whereas a USI just supplements a person's income by an amount lesser than his or her basic needs.

The minute we broach this topic we step into controversy. Why should the government hand out money which, at the end of the day, is taxpayer money, to everyone? Can the finances of the government or the country afford it? Will we simply make people dependent on handouts? Will there be no incentive left for people to work? If money has to be handed out, how much or how little should be given? These questions, and more like them, will immediately open up fissures between the political left and the political right. Their stands on each of these questions will, in all likelihood, be diametrically opposed to each other. Is it possible to find a middle ground, where we can all be not only reconciled to a policy for a USI, but be enthusiastic about? That can only happen if we are all convinced that not only do we all stand to gain from it, but that the economy too can flourish because of it. I believe that such a policy is indeed possible, and I will try to convince you of it. If we are to prosper from such a policy, it comes with a couple of riders, without which, the whole effort may turn out to be an exercise in futility. The riders, while not easy to implement, are certainly implementable.

Each country in the world is in a unique position, economically, demographically and culturally. While the general principles that I propound will be true for all, the figures, economics and the details discussed in the next two chapters will be India-specific. The numbers that I will suggest are not sacrosanct or written in stone. They are, however, in the ballpark but amenable to tweaking. Earlier in this book, whenever I have needed to write about costs and money, I have used the US dollar as the currency of reference. This was primarily because all my searches for technical advancements in various fields turned up prices in the American currency, and perhaps somewhere at the back of my mind, there was a hope that the book may find some readers outside India also.

For the USI scheme, I have decided to use Indian rupees as the currency of reference, as using the US dollar would convey little. The current exchange rate is about seventy-six rupees to the dollar. The purchasing power parity (PPP) exchange rate in 2018 was 18.10 rupees to the dollar.[1] The *Economist* magazine's Big Mac index, estimates the rupee to be 20 per cent undervalued compared to the PPP rate, putting the real exchange rate at 14.48 rupees to the dollar.[2] The Big Mac index has little relevance in India, where the vast majority of Indians has never eaten or will ever eat a Big Mac. For a USI, the index I would like to compare the value of the rupee with would be the Cost of Sustenance in Rural and Small Town Settings index. Unfortunately, such an index has never been calculated. The value of the Indian rupee, in such an index, would be close to that of an American dollar. If this sounds preposterous, I will give the example of Idli Amma.

Kamalathal is an octogenarian lady living near Coimbatore in the south Indian state of Tamil Nadu. She makes idlis (steamed rice cakes) and sells them for one rupee an idli, along with sambhar (a lentil and vegetable broth) and chutneys to go with the idlis. She is popularly known as Idli Amma or the idli Lady. Two idlis make a hot snack and three to five idlis make a hot meal. A snack of two idlis costs two rupees. An average meal of four idlis costs four rupees. At the current exchange rate, that is a hot meal for about five American cents or a nickel. Admittedly, Idli Amma sells her idlis cheaper than the rest of the market and makes very little profit. She sells about a 1,000 idlis a day but earns only about 3,000 rupees a month as she says she doesn't need more. That is why she is a legend. If she increased the price of her idlis by fifty paise, she would make 18,000 rupees a month, and the price of four idlis would increase to six rupees or about 7.5 US cents. It would still be difficult to find a hot meal in America for 6 US dollars. That is the reason I estimate that on a Rural Sustenance index, the value of an Indian rupee would be close to that of an American dollar. In such settings, the 1,000 rupees that I propose be given as the USI, will go nearly as far as 1,000 dollars in America.

I shall first state the USI scheme, which I propose, in one simple sentence and then go on to the need, reasoning and explanation of it.

The USI scheme will give to every Indian citizen, who is a resident of India and above the age of twenty-five years, including the richest Indian, a sum of 1,000 rupees every month. This money should not be added to other income for tax purposes, in effect making it tax-free in the hand of the receiver.

Reasoning:

1. The part about the scheme for every Indian citizen, who is a resident of India, needs little explanation. There is no reason for India to give this money to those who are not its citizens or those who normally reside outside India. For administrative purposes, some sort of a citizen list will need to be prepared.
2. Above the age of twenty-five years, needs some explanation. There are two reasons for this. It is no secret that many segments of our people live in conditions of unenviable poverty. If every newborn baby were to be given 1,000 rupees every month, it would, in these segments, act as an inducement to procreate. Already having the second largest

population in the world, this is not something that India needs.

The second reason is economics. India's population is a little over 1.3 billion. The median age of Indians is a little below twenty-five years, meaning that half of India's population is under twenty-five years of age and the other half over that age.[3] Accordingly, half of the population, or 650 million people, will need to be given a USI. By halving the number of recipients and at the same time ensuring an even distribution of the money across the country, it will possibly make an otherwise unaffordable scheme, affordable.

3. The richest Indian, too, should also be given the monthly USI money. He certainly does not need the money and probably does not want to take it but still, it is important that he be given it. Should we try and determine a level of income beyond which the USI should not be given, we will be entering a bureaucratic and legal quagmire, and open up half a billion points of contention. There is certainly merit in the sentiment that why should money be given to rich people in what is essentially a poverty alleviation scheme, and I wholeheartedly agree with that sentiment. The money given away to the rich, and a little more, should be taken back from the richer people by tweaking income tax rates for them. For small businesses, all years are not the same. They can close down as has happened to many small businesses during the current pandemic. If such a scheme were in operation now, it would have greatly alleviated their misery as that of daily wage earners, without the government and the newly unemployed, having to worry about child malnutrition and deaths caused by starvation.
4. What is the rationale behind the figure of 1,000 rupees per month? The average household size in India, both rural and urban, is five persons per family. Keeping in mind that half the population is above the age of twenty-five, on an average, each

household will have 2.5 persons above the age of twenty-five and receive an average of 2,500 rupees per month or 30,000 rupees a year. This amount, as a USI, is a reasonable sum in the Indian context.

The first part of this book has looked at developments in various industries. We have seen that there is likely to be a shortage of jobs in a few years. It is my thinking that a USI scheme can, if taken advantage of by providing the right conditions, become a very large creator of jobs, in both the formal and the informal sectors.

If half of India's 1.3 billion people, or 650 million people receive 1,000 rupees every month, it amounts to 650 billion rupees, or 65,000 crore rupees every month or 7,800 billion every year. In Indian nomenclature, that is 7.8 lakh crore rupees a year, and is a considerable amount of money. In the next chapter, I will examine the affordability and funding of the scheme. In this chapter, I would like to follow the money and see where it will go and what it can accomplish and if it is a worthwhile objective to pursue.

To follow the money, it would help to have a grainier picture of India. Two-thirds of Indian population is rural and one third is urban. The rural or village population is 867 million. To put this number in perspective, our village population is more than the total population of the next three most populous nations, namely, the US, Indonesia and Brazil combined. What happens in our villages is crucial to the economic well-being of India.

According to the 2011 census, India has 593,615 inhabited villages.[4] That gives us an average village with 1,460 people living in it. At five people to a household, it would mean there are, on an average, 292 households in a village. Let us round off the figure to 300 households—300 households would bring in, as USI money, 750,000 rupees to the village every month. This is in addition to whatever money is already coming to the village. What the village will do with the money is not a pertinent question. The money will not come to the village or its headman. The money will go to the bank accounts of 750 individuals. What they will each do with the money is the pertinent question.

India's 1.3 billion people range economically from the very rich to the abysmally poor. This is true of all countries, but being a comparatively poor country, we have far more poor people as a ratio, than is true of wealthier countries. The very poor in our country, have difficulty making their ends meet. But they do. The very fact that there are over 1.3 billion of us is witness to the reality that no matter how impoverished they are, they manage to keep body and soul together. However, rather than live, they subsist. Imagine that into each subsistence-level household of five members, an additional 2,500 rupees starts coming in every month. What would they do with the money? There are only three things that can be done with money. It can only be saved, invested or spent.

It is impossible to second guess how each of the 650 million recipients would spend their money. However, we can generalize. A standard way of estimating the behaviour of a large number of people is to break them into five quintiles and then try and understand how each quintile would behave. This approach is not very helpful in the case of India. If we were to plot a graph of the number of people on the horizontal axis against income on the vertical axis, it would be nearly a flat line, rising almost imperceptibly, nearly up to the end, where it would rise very steeply. This is an indicator of our high level of inequality. Income taxpayers underline this fact. Of India's 1.3 billion people, less than 15 million pay any income tax at all. That is less than 1.15 per cent[5] of India's population.

Let us get back to our average village. Villages in India are seldom affluent places. Villagers in a typical Indian village range from the very poor to the modestly comfortable. All of them have many unmet aspirations. Once they start receiving the money in their bank accounts and realize that the money will be coming every month, little of the money would be saved or invested. It would be spent. At their slightly differing economic levels, individuals would first spend their money on what each wants the most, from food to clothes to perhaps a TV, fridge or phone. It does not matter much what it would be spent on, what matters is that it would be spent. Savings would probably be discouraged at lower economic levels because an unending stream of money coming into a household every month would provide security and fulfil a major function of savings.

A few intrepid individuals, sensing rising demand, would start their own ventures. It could be anything, from a tea stall to a small grocery shop, a beauty parlour or anything they think could make a profit. These new ventures would have come into being both from rising demand as well as the venturesome nature of their promoters and their risk-taking ability. Risk-taking ability will increase if there is a constant stream of money coming in.

Let us follow the money coming into the average village a little further. When money is spent, it can be spent on either tradable goods or non-tradable goods. Tradable goods are goods that can be taken from one place to another and be sold or traded there. Examples are a factory-made pack of biscuits, a toothpaste tube or a TV. These items can be manufactured in one place and traded hundreds of miles away from where the manufacture took place. Getting a haircut or a massage, or hiring someone to do housekeeping jobs are non-tradable goods. They can only be done locally. Getting someone to paint a house is a mixture of the two. The paint is probably not manufactured in the village, but the labour for the painting is local and non-tradable.

The money spent on non-tradable goods stays within the village and gets added to the money flow into the village. If 1,000 rupees are spent on say, a person doing a housekeeping job, that is 1,000 additional rupees in that person's hand, enhancing his buying power and creating a job in the process. The extra money in the hand of the person doing the work creates further demand.

When money is spent on tradable goods manufactured outside the village but purchased within the village, the money, which accrues to the cash flow of the village, is only the gross profit of the trader, normally between 10 and 25 per cent of the price of the goods. If, instead of buying a factory-made pack of cookies, the local baker's cookies, or idlis or samosas are bought, most of the money will be retained in the village and will recirculate repeatedly. There is merit in the statement that buying local is better for the local economy. This is as true for a village economy as a national economy. This repeated circulation of money, kick-started by the infusion of money coming regularly into the village or any community, is known as the Local Multiplier Effect (LME).

Before continuing with the LME, I would like to give a little more detail about Indian villages. About 1,500 people in an average Indian village is too small a number to represent the microcosm of a functioning economy. There are just not enough people to represent enough trades to let it function as one. However, Indian villages are hardly ever stand-alone entities in the wilderness. They exist in clusters, often in walking distance to the neighbouring one, and are centred about a main village or town in the area. When I speak about the local village economy, I refer to this local cluster, which has several thousand inhabitants.

The LME is a very valuable, hidden feature of our economies. The term refers to how many times money is recirculated within a local economy before leaving through the purchase of something from outside the community, or in savings and investment instruments, operated from outside the community. The term 'Local Multiplier Effect', was first used by John Maynard Keynes, in his 1936 book, *The General Theory of Employment, Interest and Money*.[6] Keynes envisaged government spending through public works to kick-start the economy and create demand which other businesses could fulfil by hiring more people and thereby, increasing employment. The LME came back into prominence when Enrico Moretti, a professor of economics at the University of California, Berkeley, in his book, *The New Geography of Jobs*, gave an example of job creation. Apple, Moretti says, employs 13,000 people directly in Cupertino but has spurred 70,000 jobs in the region. Two-thirds of the jobs are in the local service sector, he writes and 'the almost magical economics of job creation' are that 'for each new high-tech job in the city, five additional jobs are ultimately created outside of the high-tech sector in that city, both in skilled occupations (lawyers, teachers, nurses) and in unskilled ones (waiters, hairdressers, carpenters).'[7]

I think that by 'high-tech jobs,' Moretti meant highly paid jobs. It should make no difference to a doctor or a hairdresser, if the customer was a highly skilled computer scientist or a mechanical engineer as long as he or she was able to pay their bills. Other studies done in different parts of the world, with one notable exception, have validated Moretti's findings. The exception is studies conducted in Italy, using the same methodology as Moretti, which concluded that, in Italy, there was no evidence of the LME for the creation of tradable jobs on the rest of the local economy. The study found the LME to be zero and occasionally, negative in all regions of Italy.[8] In the only explanation that could be given to explain this discrepancy, the authors point to excessive government regulation in the non-tradable sector, the government's role in wage setting, and barriers to labour mobility. This exception is relevant to India and I will return to it later in more detail, when we explore the ways by which the LME can be enhanced.

All the studies on the LME done so far have been about new jobs coming into a community or a region and bringing an inflow of money into that area which, when spent, encourages the creation of more jobs in that area. No studies have been done anywhere about a little money coming into the hands of many, and the jobs that money will create when spent. The reason why no such studies have been done is that there never has been such a scenario to study. A nationwide USI has never before been implemented. In the absence of any data, all we can do is try and reason through the steps and try to follow the money in our minds and see where it will get us.

Certainly, 1,000 rupees coming into the hands of one individual will not create five jobs, or even one job. However, 1,000 rupees coming into the hands of ten people, under conditions which encourage the maximizing of the LME, has the potential to create one job. The USI scheme, which I am advocating, envisages giving 1,000 rupees each to 650 million people every month. This money can, with the right conditions, create 65 million jobs. With the coming shortage of jobs, owing to technological developments in nearly all spheres, as discussed in the first part of this book, now further aggravated by the coronavirus crises, we owe it to ourselves to study the possibility of creating 65 million jobs in depth and then to act upon it.

While there is little evidence to suggest that governments the world over, are acutely seized by the looming threat to jobs caused by technology, they are all concerned about getting their economies working again after the devastation caused by the coronavirus. They are all either setting aside or preparing to print huge amounts of money to deal with it. Experts are recommending measures, such as refinancing banks, foregoing debts, financing corporates so that they can keep paying salaries, cutting down tax rates and a host of other measures. The predominant logic is that, if the banks and corporates can be made to weather the crisis, the benefits would also accrue to their customers and employees in the course of time.

The actions proposed by the experts are mostly versions of trickle-down economics, also called the trickle-down theory. This refers to the economic proposition that taxes on businesses and the wealthy in society should be reduced as a means to stimulate business investment in the short term and benefit society at large in the long term. The theory also implies that in times of crisis, monetary help should also be given to corporates, banks and other financial institutions. The trickle-down theory is strongly linked to supply-side economic policies. Whereas supply-side economics favours lowering taxes overall, the trickle-down theory, more specifically, advocates the lowering of taxes on the upper end of the economic spectrum.

The idea of trickle-down economics has always had its critics, even before the term was coined. In 1896, Democratic presidential candidate William Jennings Bryan described the concept in a speech, 'There are two ideas of government. There are those who believe that if you just legislate to make the well-to-do prosperous, that their prosperity will leak through on those below. The democratic idea has been that if you legislate to make the masses prosperous, their prosperity will find its way up, and through every class that rests upon it.'[9]

American humourist Will Rogers, who also seems to have been an astute observer, coined the term 'trickle-down policy' in 1932. He had this to say about American President Herbert Hoover, who presided during the Great Depression, regarding his policy of cutting taxes for higher earners and businesses. 'The money was all appropriated for the top in the hopes it will trickle down to the needy. Mr Hoover was an engineer. He knew that water trickles down. Put it uphill and let it go and it will reach the driest little spot. But he didn't know that money trickled up. Give it to the people at the bottom and the people at the top will have it before night, anyhow. But it will at least have passed through the poor fellow's hand.'[10]

Money in the hands of the needy creates demand. Money in the hands of the rich does not create immediate demand. It sometimes finds its way into tax havens, as we in India, are all too painfully aware. Even when used legitimately, it is used to buy stocks and shares and controlling interests in other companies, thereby increasing inequality. Money in the hands of the needy will soon find its way uphill into the hands of the rich through the goods and services they or their companies provide, but along the way, it will have uplifted and provided employment to the entire country.

The current situation, where jobs are being lost, both due to advances in technology and the ravages of the lockdown caused by the coronavirus, is one of a lack of demand and a cash flow problem for our businesses as their costs continue to be incurred and sales have plummeted. The government has taken many meaningful steps to mitigate the cash flow problem by steps such as deferring taxes and making credit more readily available. We are not facing a supply-side crisis. Our factories are running at a fraction of their capacities. We are facing a demand side crisis with millions of people having lost their means of livelihood and their buying power. A USI scheme, dispersed through hundreds of millions of hands, addresses the demand side of the equation directly. Such a scheme will also create jobs.

There are many types of jobs. Many of us think of jobs as nine to five employment, or in eight-hour shifts, with benefits such as sick leave and maternity leave and with pensions when we retire. Such jobs are going to be fewer in the future and eventually become rare. Most new jobs that will be created will be in the service sector of the economy. Many will be gig jobs, doable when available. Millions of Indians are already dependent on gig jobs. In all our cities, there are many places where people with various skills, like carpenters, plumbers, bricklayers or just plain helpers, congregate every morning with the hope of being picked up for a job. Are these people employed or unemployed?

The increasingly transient nature of employment will require, apart from a USI scheme, a robust self-financed, long-term savings and old age security plan. In my earlier book, *The Economic Reactor*, I have suggested one such inflation-protected plan, which will not require the government to spend on it and also act as an inducement for people to pay income taxes, by linking deposits into the savings plan with taxes paid by individuals.[11]

There are many definitions of unemployment. The official

National Sample Survey Organization (NSSO) uses two measurements of unemployment based on the Usual Status and the Current Weekly Status. The Current Weekly Status approach to measuring unemployment uses seven days preceding the date of survey as the reference period. A person is considered employed, if he or she pursues any one or more gainful activities for at least one hour on any day of the reference week. A person, in other words, is statistically employed, if he or she has worked for an hour in seven days.[12] This is reminiscent of the saying popularized by Mark Twain, 'There are lies, damned lies and statistics.' Perhaps if we reduce the definition of employment period to half an hour or even fifteen minutes a week, our unemployment figures would plummet further. The reality is worse than what the NSSO figures say. There is a high rate of concealed unemployment in Indian villages. In concealed unemployment, it is difficult to identify an unemployed person. This type of unemployment is also called, disguised unemployment. According to the UN Committee of Experts, 'The disguisedly unemployed are the persons who work on their own account and who are too numerous relatively to resources.' If a certain task can, for example, be done by three persons, but five persons claim to be doing it, two are disguisedly unemployed. Disguised unemployment in rural India is 25 per cent to 30 per cent.[13] Even by the liberal description of employment for one hour a week being considered employment, the unemployment figures have been rising sharply even before the coronavirus epidemic.

According to NSSO findings, between 2011–12 and 2017–18, that is in a period of six years, the increase in the unemployment rate is more than three times among rural men and more than double among rural women. In the case of urban men and women, it has doubled. This is the creeping unemployment we can expect because of technological advances. The lockdown has exacerbated the job losses. We do not, as yet, know how many millions of jobs have been or will be lost. Some of us may be harbouring the thought that once a vaccine or other cure is discovered for the virus, things will go back to as they were before the onset of the virus. I do not think that is how events will play out. To a large extent, we are creatures of habit. Once we are forced by events to break those habits, we are more likely to form new habits rather than to go back to the old ones. Because we have been precluded, by the lockdown, from interacting with each other physically, relying instead on digital interactions and video conferencing, these may become our new habits, reinforced by the fact that the new habits save both time and money. I expect digital businesses to grow at the cost of brick and mortar businesses. Companies will discover that they can perform just as well with fewer employees. Employment levels in each company will never recover to the same extent as before. Unemployment will increase on a long-term basis.

This is not a time for incremental policy changes. This is firefighting time. This is the time to assuage the immediate hardships of millions and to encourage the rapid creation of jobs. A USI scheme under the right conditions can do both. It is impossible to overemphasize the necessity that a USI scheme should create jobs. If such a scheme cannot create jobs, it is a dead duck in the water. It will do more harm than good. If the number of jobs, and hence the number of goods and services available in the market, remain the same, it can only lead to inflation. Considering the large sums of money that will be put into people's hands, the inflation can be severe. The creation of jobs will depend on how we can strengthen the factors that lead to job creation.

To try and estimate the number of jobs that are likely to be created, because of the USI scheme, I will be looking at the different factors that can impede the creation of jobs and estimate the extent to which each of these factors, in a given situation and background will deter job creation. Rather than look at jobs directly, I will be estimating the effect of each factor on the LME and then calculate the number of jobs which can be created. For each of the factors that can retard job creation, I will try to estimate a numerical value for the extent to which each factor can retard job creation and call it the LME multiplier for that particular factor. If a particular factor in a given situation has no detrimental effect on job creation, it will have an LME multiplier of 1. If another factor does not permit any jobs to be created, it will have an LME multiplier of 0, indicating that no matter how favourable all the other factors are, no jobs at all will be created. There is only one factor that I can think of, which can go all the way down to zero. It is the law and order multiplier. In a state of total anarchy, the LME can go all the way down to 0.

While calculating the jobs likely to be created in an average village and the country as a whole, the LME multipliers for each factor or variable can be different from the village to the country. For estimating the value of LME multipliers for the average village and the number of jobs likely to be created there, I have used the figures as applicable to the village, but visualized the economic interactions happening in the cluster of villages around a small town, where local jobs can be located. I am aware that the value of each of these multipliers will be challenged and I would welcome that. Pending extensive research by economists and sociologists, these estimates will remain just that—estimates. The final validation of these estimates can only happen when the scheme is implemented, and the results observed.

There are eight variables in all which will impact the effect of the LME on job creation. Let us examine each of them and try to understand how they impact job creation and at the same time try to estimate the extent of the impact by estimating an LME multiplier for each variable. Through this approach, I believe, a formula can be evolved to estimate job creation anywhere, where new money is coming in. Certainly, the LME multipliers can be significantly different from place to place, but the approach should work.

The first variable is the amount of new money, which comes into the community or the country. This is the basic figure, which we do not need to estimate. We know this figure. Our average village of 300 households will receive 750,000 rupees every month and the nation as a whole will receive 65,000 crore rupees every month. Our rich people who comprise less than 1 per cent of the population and who will have a net outflow of money under the USI scheme, are numerically small enough to be ignored for these calculations. For the funding of the scheme, however, where they will contribute significantly, they cannot be ignored at all.

The second variable is the proportion of money spent locally. In a perfect world (purely from a job creation perspective), if all the money was spent on local services and local people were prepared to provide those services, all the money received would contribute to the LME and keep creating jobs, until there aren't any more people to take up the jobs and there was full employment. However, that is not the world we live in. All our needs and wants cannot be met through local services. We need material and tradable goods too.

In the case of the village, any savings or investments made in banks or other institutions having their control centres outside the local area, would not contribute to the LME. I am not in any way deriding savings. Savings are important both for an individual as well as a community but are not part of the village LME. In the case of the country as a whole, savings and investments made in Indian banks and institutions would contribute to the national LME if the banks put the money to use in India.

In the case of the village, not many tradable goods are likely to be manufactured in the local area. The only money that would go towards contributing to the LME would be the money spent on local services and goods made or grown in the village. The gross margin a trader makes, when selling tradable goods procured from outside the local area and sold locally, would also contribute to the LME. Not having any realistic idea as to how much money is spent on local goods and services, I will assume that half or 0.5 of the money is spent on local goods and services. This gives us an LME multiple of 0.5 to be applied to the initial amount.

In the case of the country as a whole, we have better data. In 2018, India's imports were 23.64 per cent of its GDP.[14] In addition to this, Indians spend a great deal of money holidaying abroad and for education in foreign universities, all of which are not fully captured in the import figures. The total portion of our GDP, which is spent outside the country, is more likely closer to 30 per cent, indicating that 70 per cent is spent within the country. For the country as a whole, this gives us an LME multiplier of 0.7 for our calculations.

The prime minister is quite right in exhorting Indians to holiday in India rather than abroad. That would directly impact the LME. In 2018, Indian tourists spent 6.5 lakh crore rupees. Of this about 1.52 lakh crore, close to one per cent of GDP, was spent in holidaying abroad.[15] This money was not part of any multiplier effect for India. India has also performed miserably in attracting foreign tourists. By the same measure, had we been able to attract significant foreign tourists to spend in India, their spending would have become part of our LME. In my last book, *The Economic Reactor*, I have examined tourism in some detail and recommend it to anyone interested in tourism in India.[16] I cannot, however, refrain from adding a little comment about Goa. Goa had, over the years, earned for itself a reputation as the prime tourist destination not only in India, but also in all of South Asia. Goa was blessed with beautiful beaches, but more than that it had a laid-back atmosphere, with music and dancing on the beaches until late in the night. It was an enjoyable experience and tourists from around the world and India went there in sizable numbers. Then things started changing. Curbs were put on alcohol on the beaches and the hours the restaurants could stay open, perhaps out of a sense of morality. In contrast, Sri Lanka actively started attracting tourists. They started building beach resorts without the prohibitions. As late as 2009, tourist arrivals in Sri Lanka were as little as 450,000. By 2018, their tourist arrivals were over 2.33 million, with nearly half a million coming from India.[17] If we choose to be moralistic and think of people having a good time as somehow being wrong, we can do so. But we cannot expect that there will be no consequences of our actions. It is not enough that there be points of interest in a country to attract visitors. Efforts have to be made to ensure that visitors, including our own citizens, have a pleasant experience in our country.

The third variable is what I call the permissiveness multiplier. If there are activities that earn money the world over but are either prohibited or frowned upon for cultural or political reasons, they reduce the permissiveness multiplier. If all activities were easily possible to venture into, the multiplier would be 1. The more activities that are prohibited the lower will be this multiplier. In most Indian villages, a tavern would not be permitted. Indeed in some Indian states, where there is a prohibition on the sale and consumption of alcohol, no tavern may open anywhere in the state, decreasing both the permissiveness multiplier and revenues for the state. This is also true of live entertainment in the form of singers, dancers or any other kinds of performers. India has an abundance of talent as witnessed by the popularity of many talent shows on television. In a more permissive background, the talent would bring job opportunities. It is not much different in the cities and the rest of the country. Many activities, before they can be started, need to deal with stringent conditions and require clearances from multiple departments, including the police, with the attendant harassment of an intending entrepreneur. They are often subject to high licence fees. All of this deters the opening up of businesses, the creation of jobs and a diminishing of the LME. It is difficult to calculate the permissiveness multiplier, but I estimate it to be 0.6 for the average village and 0.7 for the country as a whole.

The fourth variable is the resistance to let women work. If

women cannot be a part of the labour pool, it will slow down job growth, as there will be fewer people to take up jobs. A few decades ago, social barriers against women working were considerable. In urban India, there is now little resistance to women working. In the villages, it is still there to some extent. I estimate the women's work multiplier to be 0.7 for the average village and to be 0.8 for the country as a whole. The women's work multiplier can never go below 0.5. If no women work, all work will not stop. This model assumes that all men are willing to work. Women, being only half the potential workforce, can only bring down the multiplier to 0.5 if none of them is willing or permitted to work.

The fifth variable is the ease with which a small business can be started and run. I emphasize on the small—1,000 rupees a month, coming into the hands of hundreds of millions of people, will create demand in the economy, but in the beginning, it will be a demand for small things. As jobs are created and wealth increases both totally and in individual hands, the demand for larger and more expensive goods will increase. Recently when the World Bank's Doing Business 2020 report was released, India's ranking improved from 77 to 63 which signifies a substantial improvement. However, this report has absolutely no bearing on the ease of doing business in villages and small towns in India.

One assumption that the World Bank index makes is the location of a standardized business—the subject of doing a business case study—in the largest business city of the economy. Starting with Doing Business 2015, coverage was extended also to the second-largest cities for economies having more than 100 million people. In the case of India, the studies conducted so far are of small, medium and large businesses in Mumbai and Delhi. After 2020, the index intends to include Bengaluru and Kolkata. Also, the standardized case scenario usually involves a limited liability company or its legal equivalent.[18, 19] None of the case studies that may have been done in Mumbai and Delhi of limited liability companies can have any relevance to small businesses in villages and small towns.

The World Bank's index covers ten areas of doing business, starting with 'Starting a business' and ending with 'Resolving insolvency'. The index also includes areas such as minority shareholder interests, approval of building plans, registering property, trading across borders and getting electricity connections. None of these are of major concern to the village or small-town entrepreneur. Regrettably, the ease of paying taxes is also of no concern to them. The only parameters that would be of interest to her or him are getting credit and the enforcement of contracts. The USI scheme could help, to a large extent, in solving small-scale credit. A family could, for instance, be allowed to pledge their USI incoming money for a limited period of about five years, to finance capital purchases to start a business. The money could be given directly to the bank as monthly instalments. As there would be no risk involved for the bank, it could be treated as sovereign debt with the lowest possible interest rate.

All in all, it is not very difficult to start and run a small business in our villages and small towns. These small businesses go below the radar of bureaucratic surveillance and control. A village entrepreneur has only to keep the local minions of the state in good humour. I estimate the multiplier for the ease of doing business in the average village to be 0.9.

It is a different story for our towns and cities and for larger projects. These come under the scrutiny of bureaucrats from a variety of departments, often armed with archaic laws that have long outlived the purpose they were created for. I will refrain from going into any of these laws, because that will require a book at least twice as long as this one and a knowledge of the law, which I simply do not have. The general perception, however, is that a law can be found for preventing any conceivable initiative. Even if the law, which is dragged out to prohibit a certain initiative, does not exactly fit the situation, by the time the case has run the gamut of legal procedures, a decade or two may pass. This is unfortunate. The changing world, which is rushing towards us, will require new thinking and new solutions else we will be headed towards chaos. The current pandemic should have brought home to us the urgency of needing innovative solutions when jobs vanish.

With the situation as it now exists, I estimate the LME multiplier because of the ease of doing business for city-based middle-sized or large business ventures to be 0.6.

Before I move on from the ease of doing business variable to the next one, I would like to share a few thoughts about our bureaucracy and our legal processes. The average Indian regards the bureaucracy as part of the problem and not as part of the solution. This is a terrible waste of the country's resources. Only some of our brightest and best manage to join the civil services after arduous study and many tests. The Indian Administration Service was visualized and often referred to as the steel frame, which held the country together. Steel frames are wondrous things. They make skyscrapers possible. They make, what would otherwise be impossible, structures of all kinds possible. The steel is as good as it ever was. Somehow, policymakers have denigrated the design of the steel frames into steel cages. Bureaucrats are now rewarded if they follow rules and find reasons for preventing any development that challenges the status quo. Steel frames make the impossible, possible. Steel cages make the possible, impossible. If the reward system of the bureaucracy could be altered to include the creation of objectively measurable businesses and jobs created at every level of administration, it would go a long way in retrieving the steel frame from the steel cage.

It would be a good step to encourage the formation of companies, the major purpose of which is to act as a midwife for the birthing of new small businesses and guide them through the labyrinth of rules and regulations that bedevil small businesses for a few years. These companies could be given about 5 per cent of the new entity's profits for say, ten years as their source of revenue. A major side effect of such companies would be the realistic reporting of profits of small businesses, as the source of income for the midwife companies would depend on the profits made by the businesses they advise. The mentoring companies could each mentor many small businesses and themselves become profitable entities. These midwife companies could also be charged with the responsibility of organizing for or enrolling would-be entrepreneurs into short basic courses of perhaps a week to a month for imparting basic skills. Prospective 'samosa' or other food stall operators, for example, should be imparted basic training in hygiene and food safety before they are permitted to set up shop.

Retired bureaucrats or serving ones willing to take premature retirement could either start or join such companies. The pithy phrase, 'Set a thief to catch a thief' is wholly inappropriate. 'Set an expert to deal with an expert' is more apt, but the underlying intent to state that those with knowledge of a system are best suited to deal with it is quite clear. The way I visualize it is that an intending entrepreneur could go to one of the midwife companies with the proposed business in mind and be guided towards implementing it. The would-be entrepreneur will be taken seriously, as he or she represents a source of income for the midwife company for say ten years.

The Indian bureaucracy is a vast organization with the momentum of decades of tradition, going back to before the independence of the country. It also has the protection of parts of the Constitution. As a result, administrative reforms are not easy. In some ways, it can be likened to a fully laden supertanker moving at full speed with a great deal of momentum. It is impossible to stop the tanker or reverse it quickly. In case of an imminent collision, the only thing that can be done is to alter the course so that collision is averted. We are now at a point of an imminent collision with reality. The rapid loss of millions of jobs and no safety net is a recipe for disaster. For the first time since independence, anarchy is a distinct possibility. A USI scheme will provide the safety net. A tweaking of the rules, by rewarding the bureaucracy for encouraging job formation, will provide the course correction.

Enforcing contracts is crucial for businesses of all sizes. Businesses are carried out on the basis of contracts. Contracts are one of the most common legal transactions that are encountered while running any business. A contract may or may not be a written contract. It may not even be a spoken contract as in the case of an implied contract. If you go into a restaurant and order a dish, you have entered into an implied contract that you will pay for the dish. If you apply for a job and are accepted through a letter of appointment, that letter is a contract between you and your employer, stating what is expected of you and how you will be remunerated. When one company places an order with another company, for say, a thousand widgets at a laid-out price, it is a contract in the form of a promise to pay a certain amount upon performance of the order. A contract is always a quid pro quo agreement, where one party promises to undertake a specified action upon the performance of another specified action by the other party. Disputes arise when one party has performed its part of the contract and the other party declines to perform its part.

When one of the parties to the contract fulfils its part of the contract and the other party does not, depending upon the size of the contract, losses can be severe, leading up to even the collapse of a business. It is crucial for businesses' confidence that a quick legal remedy is available for resolving disputes and enforcing contracts. India fares very badly on this ease of doing business parameter. Singapore fares best and ranks first on this measure. On an average, it takes 164 days, or five and a half months to enforce a contract in Singapore.[20] India is ranked 163rd on this parameter and on an average, it takes 1445 days or four years, to enforce a contract in India.[21] Four years is sometimes enough to destroy a business. There are two reasons for the tardy performance of Indian courts. The first, as the judiciary claims, is that there are not enough courtrooms and judges to do the job. The second, as critics of the system claim, is that court procedures as practised, are as if they have been designed for delay. There is validity in both claims.

In the government budget for 2020–21, the total budgetary allocation for the ministry of law and justice is 2,200 crore rupees.[22] With 36 million court cases pending in all Indian courts combined,[23] it is easy to gauge how much importance we give to speedy justice, if we consider that the budget allocated to the ministry of youth affairs and sports is 2,827 crore rupees. The Umbrella Programme for Development of Scheduled Tribes has been allocated nearly two times as much with 4,191 crore and the Umbrella Scheme for Development of Scheduled Castes with three times as much as the entire justice delivery system of the country, with 6,242 crore rupees.

Court delays are taken for granted. Court delays have derisively entered the popular lexicon as *tareek pe tareek*, which translates to 'postponement after postponement with no end in sight.' If there is a date set for you to appear in court, your friends are more likely to ask you what the next date set for going to court is, rather than about the outcome of the hearing. If a court case appears to be going against one of the litigants, it is easy to get multiple postponements. Lawyers, too, are complicit in this, as they charge their full fees, even for a postponed hearing.

One piece of legislation could speed up court processes significantly. In any court case, there are three parties, namely, the prosecuting lawyer who is often the public prosecutor as the government and its departments are the largest litigants in the country, the defending lawyer and the judicial system. If it is legislated that in any case which is filed and goes to court, each of the three parties can ask for the postponement of a hearing, for up to a month, only once during the pendency of the case, free of any financial liability. Beyond this one postponement, should any of the three parties ask for a postponement or not show up for a hearing, that party will be liable for all costs, including court costs and the fees of the opposing lawyers. The individual lawyers or the law firm they represent must be personally liable for this payment and not be able to pass on the costs to their clients, unless it is on the explicit written instructions of the client, in which case the client will be responsible for the payments. Should it become apparent that one of the parties to the litigation, who is able to afford the costs and is using the postponements to delay the verdict of the case, the judge must be duty-bound to disallow the postponement and hear the case ex-parte if need be. In the case of appeals to higher courts against judgements by lower courts, time limits for filing appeals are already specified, but seldom adhered to, especially if it is a government department making the appeal. The time limits should be made inviolable. Businesses need closure of old issues, if they are to focus on future growth.

If the government intends to encourage and expedite the starting and running of new and existing businesses, it has to find the money to majorly expand the legal infrastructure and appoint more judges. There should be enough judges for some to be on stand-by, in case of the sudden inability of a judge to perform his or her duties. The aim has to be to find legal closure of all matters within a year and contract enforcement cases within six months to catch up with Singapore.

We have already seen how tardy dispute resolution has precluded the setting up of a whole business vertical, namely the hiring of cars for being driven by the hirer. Let us try and ensure that other opportunities are not lost.

If both the bureaucratic reforms listed above and the speedy resolution of contract enforcement cases is carried through, there is no reason why the LME multiplier for the country as a whole, for the variable of ease of doing business cannot move from 0.6 to

1.0. This will have a large impact on job creation, as we will see.

The sixth variable is the existing level of unemployment. If the unemployment level is high, there will be no dearth of people to take up new jobs. India currently has a high level of unemployment and does not face the problem of there being no people to take up new jobs. We have enough unemployment to go around and conditions being favourable for job creation, it will let new jobs be created. In a sense, we have to work our way up to the problem of low unemployment, where it will become a hindrance for job creation. As we have a large number of unemployed people, I estimate the LME unemployment multiplier to be 1.0 for the average village and also for the country as a whole.

The seventh variable is the law and order variable. This is the most severe variable. In a situation of total anarchy, or where war is raging, this variable can go down to zero, preventing any business activity or job creation to happen. Another way of describing the situation is that there is no security of property. Any wealth, which a person may possess, is kept hidden away and no economic activity can take place. This variable explains the situation in war-torn countries such as Libya and Syria. This multiple will also be low for countries like Afghanistan. Happily, this is not the case in India. Here there is more risk of loss of property through shortcomings in legal processes, than to looting. Accordingly, I estimate the LME multiplier for law and order to be 1.0 for both the average village and all of India at present.

Having allotted an LME multiplier of 1.0 for law and order for both the average village and all of India, I must state the obvious. This condition has not always been so for all parts of the country at all times. The main exceptions have been West Bengal during Jyoti Basu's tenure as chief minister and to a lesser extent during the tenure of Mamata Banerjee. It has also not been so in Bihar during the tenures of Laloo Yadav and Rabri Devi. It has also not been so for most of the time in Kerela. During these periods, lumpen elements of society, acting as political party cadres and militant trade unions have thwarted job creation in these places. This has caused a major exodus of talent and capital away from these areas causing job losses instead of job creation. These examples are a validation of the powerful role of the law and order LME multiplier.

The eighth and last variable is minimum wage legislation. In today's popular liberal mindset, anyone questioning minimum wage laws is seen as set to exploit labour and increase the profits of employers. That is an incomplete perception and looks at only one side of the coin. Let us conduct a small thought experiment and see the larger picture.

Imagine a talented man has taught himself to make the best samosas (a fried triangle-shaped pastry with a savoury filling) in the local area, along with the most appealing spice mix for the stuffing and excellent chutneys to go with the samosas. He sets up a small stall in the nearest marketplace and starts making and selling the samosas. Making samosas is a laborious process. It involves mixing the spices, blending them with the stuffing made of boiled potatoes and other ingredients, kneading the flour and rolling out small sheets of the dough which are then moulded into the right shape, stuffed and sealed before deep frying the samosas and selling them. Because of his excellent recipe, his samosas acquire a reputation for excellence, and he is often sold out. He is able to make 200 samosas a day and sells each samosa for five rupees, making a net profit of two rupees on each samosa, earning an income of 12,000 rupees per month. He then figures out that if he can employ a person to help him, he can increase his income.

There is an unemployed lad living in his village, and he offers a job to the lad to help him to make samosas at 5,000 rupees a month. The job is gratefully accepted. The man doubles his sales, while retaining control over his trade secrets of spice mixes and chutney recipes. The gross income now becomes 24,000 rupees, out of which the lad he has employed gets 5,000 and he himself has a take home income of 17,000 rupees. In a few months, he buys himself a motorcycle and his helper buys a bicycle, spurring demand elsewhere in the economy. In the course of time, he rents a larger place and puts in a few tables and chairs while adding a few equally good products to his menu. Because he is maintaining his quality and people are coming from nearby towns to try out his products, he contemplates opening up branches in nearby towns. This is when the weight of the Indian bureaucracy bears down upon him. Inspectors that he did not know even existed start paying regular visits. He is kept busy attending to the inspectors, filling their forms and packing samosas for them to take home. Inevitably, he loses focus on the quality of his goods, which was his responsibility solely. His legendary samosas become just samosas. After opening a few outlets in nearby towns, he gives up thoughts of further expansion. This is exactly what did not happen to Ray Kroc. Ray Kroc was the man who grew McDonald's from a single outlet to the worldwide chain it now is on the strength of the high quality of a single product, namely potato fries and also reasonably priced burgers.

There is another takeaway from the thought experiment about the intrepid samosa-maker. I refer to the bicycle that his helper buys and the motorcycle that he himself buys. The 1,000 rupees a month, initially put into the hands of millions of people may only generate a demand for low-valued goods, but the enterprise unleashed will soon cascade upwards and generate a demand for higher priced goods across the entire spectrum of goods.

Had our enterprising samosa-maker adhered to the minimum wage laws, he would not have been able to afford a helper in the first place, and the virtuous cycle of growth and increased jobs would not even start. According to the website of the chief labour commissioner of the Government of India,[24] the country is divided into three areas for the purpose of minimum wages. To quote from the website, 'Therefore, the minimum rates of wages showing the basic rates and Variable Dearness Allowance payable w.e.f 01.04.2020 shall be as under[...]'. The daily wage rates for the three areas in rupees are 629, 525 and 420. The lowest daily wage of 420 means a monthly wage of 12,600 rupees. Had our enterprising man paid heed to the minimum wage laws, he would not have been able to afford a helper in the first place. The virtuous cycle of growth and increased jobs would not even have started. He may have stayed a more content man eking out a modest living selling 200 samosas every day, but that is a personal matter. Happiness and contentment are in no way the responsibility of the government or the bureaucracy. Neither it seems are growth and employment.

As it now stands, small businesses in our average village are all in the informal sector and are not impacted by minimum wage Acts at all. They are also not impacted by other labour laws, such as the inability to lay off workers. In different parts of the country, it is possible to hire fresh inexperienced workers from villages for between 4,000 and 6,000 rupees a month. For the purpose of trying to calculate the number of jobs that are likely to be created in the average village because of the proposed USI scheme, I have used the figure of 5,000 rupees. Accordingly, I estimate the LME because of minimum wage and other labour laws to be 1.0 for the average village.

It is a somewhat more complex story for the country as a whole. No one knows for sure what percentage of Indians work in the informal sector. Various estimates put that figure above 90 per cent. The Economic Survey of 2018–2019, released on 4 July 2019, says 'almost 93 per cent' of the total workforce is informal.[25] This puts a different perspective on minimum wage Acts and labour laws in general. The detrimental effect on unemployment because of minimum wages and other labour laws is limited, because only a few adhere to those laws. As a result, it is possible for the unorganized sector, which employs over 90 per cent of all workers, to employ an inexperienced person, in towns and cities, from between 7,000 and 9,000 rupees per month and for the purpose of calculating possible job creation as a result of the USI scheme, I have used 8,000 rupees as a starting wage. Because of the high degree of employment arising from the informal sector, I estimate the LME of minimum wage and other labour policies to be a high 0.8. Had all employment been in the formal sector, my estimate would have been considerably lower.

The difference of 3,000 rupees between the lowest acceptable wage in a village and a city is explained by the cost of living for a person from rural India, when he or she goes to a city to look for a job. The yardstick a migrant worker typically uses is the amount of money that can be sent back to the family in the village. The conditions that an average migrant worker endures are often unpleasant with four or even more people cramped into one small room. The reason he or she leaves the village is because there is no job available in the village that pays even 5,000 rupees. This will change once a USI scheme is implemented and jobs become available near where they live.

There is no denying the fact that minimum wage Acts depress employment. In an attempt to see how minimum wages could impact job creation, I have also calculated for their effect on employment by using the middle figure of 525 rupees per day as advocated by the chief labour commissioner—525 rupees a day adds up to 15,750 rupees a month. The reason I focus on minimum wages and not median wages is because that is the level at which the bulk of new job creation takes place. Minimum wage acts are irrelevant to highly qualified college graduates or people with valuable experience. India has over 5 million software engineers, all of them earning well above any minimum wage. Their wages are not protected by any Act, but by the laws of supply and demand and the value they deliver to their employers.

Recently, some state governments in India have realized the detrimental effect that labour laws have on employment. The realization has been spurred by the urgency to find jobs for the millions of workers returning to their home states after being rendered jobless or without a source of income due to the economic mayhem caused by the coronavirus. Uttar Pradesh, India's most populous state and Madhya Pradesh, another large state, have suspended many labour laws, including laws that prevented employers from laying off workers when needed.[26] Curiously, they have omitted removing minimum wage laws, which should have been the first to go to spur job creation.

Summarized below are the variables on which job creation is dependent when new money comes into a community. The amounts and the estimated LME multipliers for each of the variables, for both the average village and for all of India, are also stated.

Variables	*LME Multipliers*	
	Village	*All India*
Monthly incoming money In Rupees	750,000	650,000,000,000
Buying Local	0.5	0.7
Permissiveness	0.6	0.7
Women's Participation	0.7	0.8
Ease of Doing Business	0.9	0.6
Rate of Unemployment	1.0	1.0
Law and Order	1.0	1.0
Minimum Acceptable Wage In Rupees	5,000	8,000

Using these figures, calculating likely employment generation is fairly straightforward. All we need to do is to multiply the incoming money by each of the multipliers and then to divide the resultant figure by the minimum acceptable wage.

On doing these simple calculations, we find that the number of jobs likely to be generated, in the average village of 300 households will be twenty-eight. The number of jobs likely to be generated across the country, with the multiples postulated for the country as a whole, is 15.288 million. To underline the impact of each multiple, I have done two more calculations, changing only one variable in each. In the first, I have changed the multiple for the Ease of Doing Business for the all-India multiple from 0.6 to 1.0, assuming the changes discussed earlier, regarding the refocusing of the bureaucracy and speedy contract enforcement measures are carried out. The likely job creation in that case will rise from 15.288 million to 25.480 million. That is an increase of over 10 million jobs. In the second, I have assumed that the minimum wages, already decreed by the labour ministry, are rigidly enforced across the country. The minimum acceptable wage will then increase from 8,000 rupees to 15,750 rupees, which is the mid-level wage, decreed by the ministry. The likely job creation will then drop from 15.288 million to 7.765 million.

These likely job creation figures are just the beginning. The magic of job creation because of the LME does not end here. This is merely the first cycle of job creation. We have seen that twenty-eight jobs have been created in our average village. Twenty-eight jobs, paying 5,000 rupees each, amounts to 140,000 rupees. This additional amount will have the same kind of impact on jobs as the original 750,000 rupees. The amount coming into the village now becomes 890,000 and applying the same calculations will generate an additional thirty-three jobs, taking the number of total jobs created to sixty-one after the second cycle. This increase of jobs will continue cycle after cycle. After five cycles, a total of 204 additional jobs will have been created in the village of 300 households, because of the USI scheme and the effects of the LME. Similarly, the cumulative number of jobs that could be created in the whole country after five cycles of the LME will be in excess of 110 million.

This presents us with two questions regarding the LME cycles, namely, how long an LME cycle is and if the cycles can continue generating jobs indefinitely. There are no distinct cycles, in the sense that when the first one ends, the second begins. It is a continuous process, evolving imperceptibly, changing not only the job figures but also the LME multipliers. At the same time, what happens in the second or subsequent cycles is dependent on the jobs created in the preceding cycles. It is not as if all the twenty-eight jobs in the first cycle have to be created before the second cycle starts. In a way, there will be many concurrent cycles in progress at any time. However, cycles help us to think out the cause and effect of newly created jobs, generating more jobs. It also helps us to calculate the jobs that it may be possible to generate under specific conditions. The length of such a cycle is highly variable and depends almost entirely on the Ease of Doing Business. Purely as a guess, I would state that an LME cycle could be as small as six months or take years. The Ease of Doing Business is important not only for creating the first jobs but also for the speed of further job formation.

The LME will not continue generating jobs indefinitely. The LME multipliers we have used to calculate the jobs that might be created, will change. As more jobs are created and taken up, the unemployment multiplier will drop from 1.0 that we had estimated earlier, slowing down future job creation to some extent. Because there will then be no great surplus of labour, the minimum acceptable wage will rise in both our average village as well as the country as a whole. There will be no minimum wage laws or labour inspectors needed to enforce minimum wages. Reducing unemployment figures and prosperity will ensure that wages rise.

With rising prosperity, the very social fabric of society will begin to change. Society may become more permissive, increasing the permissiveness multiplier, or more orthodox, lowering the multiplier. Women may become more willing to participate in the labour force, or they may see less reason to do so, changing that multiplier one way or the other. The point being that the multipliers that we have used so far, are in no way sacrosanct or permanent. They are nothing but a reflection of the reality on the ground. They will need to be periodically reviewed to reflect that reality.

This methodology of first determining the LME multipliers before calculating the jobs that may be created, gives preponderance to the weakest link in the chain of factors that determine job creation. It may take many factors to successfully generate jobs, but it will take just one unfavourable factor to preclude the possibility of new jobs, as in the case of war-torn countries. It is of not much help if one or two multipliers are high and the rest abysmal.

At this point, I must give a word of caution against the calculations I have used to guess future employment figures as also against traditional economic thinking. A modern economy is not a linear system but a dynamic system. If a policy change or other external event, affects one parameter of the economy, that change will induce changes in other parameters. Linear equations cannot depict the reality on the ground or of dynamic systems generally. Dynamic systems, where the change of one variable causes other variables to change over time, are notoriously difficult for mathematicians to calculate. Computer modelling is used to depict the changes that will ensue with the change of one parameter. This book proposes a radical change in three parameters namely, the infusion of some money at every point of the economy, a dramatic improvement in the Ease of Doing Business in village and small-town levels and a quick dispute resolution system. It will take a very high level of competence to construct a computer model of the changes to come.

If some money is taken away from existing welfare schemes to fund the USI, and some additional money is also used through deficit financing for the scheme, economists may be tempted to do a simple ratio proportion calculation to determine the additional jobs that will be created, based on the money spent and the jobs being created currently. That is not how dynamic systems work.

Economists are familiar with the term Lorenz Curve,[27] which is the graphical depiction of income inequality or wealth inequality. It was developed by American economist Max Lorenz in 1905. They are not as familiar with the terms, Lorenz equations and Lorenz attractor.[28] These were solutions developed by American mathematician Edward Lorenz to depict how small changes in dynamical systems could affect the overall system in very major ways. The computer modelling of his equations suggested that a dynamic system would never settle down completely but with time could oscillate about a pattern called the Lorenz attractor. Interestingly, the computer representation showed the attractor to resemble butterfly wings. This gave rise to the term Butterfly Effect, popularly understood as a butterfly flapping its wings in one part of the world may cause a cyclone somewhere else.

The changes suggested here could well lead to an attractor, which oscillates about a point near full employment. These changes will not be easy to implement, but each tiny improvement will yield results far out of proportion to what a small change would accomplish in a linear system.

The benefits that a USI scheme can deliver are too great to ignore. I can only hope that decision makers consider it.

Let us now see if we can afford a Universal Supplementary Scheme.

11

INDIA CAN AFFORD A USI SCHEME

It is a general perception that Universal Basic Income or Universal Supplementary Income schemes are expensive and if affordable at all, it is only by very affluent countries. This perception is not necessarily always true. India, I believe, is ideally positioned to afford and benefit from such a scheme.

Before I go on to discuss the affordability of the USI plan, I would like to discuss the word 'expensive'. A car costing two crore rupees is an expensive car, but a ship costing two crore is a cheap ship. A ship costing 200 crore rupees is an expensive ship, but that amount is dirt cheap for an aircraft carrier. The word 'expensive' is a comparative word. An article or a plan to spend a certain amount of money can only be termed cheap or expensive depending on what one gets for the money. The USI scheme has the potential to create tens of millions of new jobs. It can alleviate extreme deprivation and the threat of hunger and malnutrition for hundreds of millions of Indians. It can act as a safety net as we do our own trapeze acts to improve our condition in life. As the country is reeling from the effects of the coronavirus and the slowing of the economy due to the effects of the lockdown, the scheme will also play a major role in restarting economic activity. At a cost of 7.8 lakh crore a year, it is not an expensive scheme. However, we still need to see if we can find the money to implement it.

India has three major advantages, not shared by most countries, when it comes to implementing the scheme, as I have described it. India also has one major disadvantage, again not shared by most countries when it comes to reaping the benefits of the scheme.

Our first major advantage is that we are largely a family-oriented culture. We do not abandon our children and wash our hands of the responsibility of looking out for them as soon as they are eighteen years old. In a pinch, the extended family also steps in with a helping hand. It is for this reason that we can delay making the monthly payments to our young people until they are twenty-five years of age. Young people may think it to be unfair that money is not going into their bank accounts every month, but we can only do what is financially possible for the nation to do. In any case, with additional money going into their families, with no reciprocity demanded of them, their condition can only improve.

India's second major advantage is that we are a low-maintenance people. Our costs are low. Our typical diets do not cost very much. When I say this, the segments of people I have in mind are mostly in the villages and also in the slums of our cities. (The 2011 census identified 13.8 million households in city slums, which at five persons per household is 69 million people.[1]) These are the people who need a helping hand the most and constitute the vast majority of Indians. The rich Indians spend as passionately as anyone else, but they do not fit into this equation at all, except as contributors to some extent for the funds needed for it. The money which will be given to them by one hand, namely through the USI, will be taken away along with a little more by the other hand, namely through higher taxes.

We are looking at a sum of 1,000 rupees a month given to half our people to make a large difference in our well-being, prosperity and economic growth. The nominal value of 1,000 rupees at the current exchange rate of seventy-six rupees to the US dollar is USD 13.15. That is less than the hourly minimum wages in some American states. We are indeed a low-cost nation and better positioned to execute such a scheme than many other nations, which are perceived to be better off.

Our third major advantage is that we have a plethora of well-meaning but ill-conceived and ill-administered schemes to help various sections of our poor. Many of these schemes can be dismantled forthwith, and the money saved, used to fund putting money into the hands of people directly.

The Mahatma Gandhi National Rural Employment Guarantee Act (MGNREGA) is the flagship poverty alleviation scheme of the central government. It aims to enhance livelihood security in rural areas by providing at least 100 days of wage employment in a financial year to every household whose adult members volunteer to do unskilled manual work. The programme has not quite lived up to its promise. A report sought by activist Dinesh Chadha, under the Right to Information Act, revealed that about 131.7 million people were registered under the MGNREGA in Fiscal Year (FY) 2018. Out of these, only 57.3 million sought work and only 51.1 million were given work. Only 2.96 million workers got full 100 days of work. The reply by the ministry also disclosed that the unemployment allowance, which is required by the Act to be given if no employment can be provided, was given to a total of 217 persons. As per the official numbers available on the MGNREGA website, in FY18, the average days of employment provided per household was 45.77. Late wage payments make the scheme unattractive to workers. A study done by Azim Premji University has found that 78 per cent of payments were not made on time.

Corruption is also rife in the administration of the scheme. In 2012, a scam was uncovered in Karnataka where one million fake job cards were detected, which resulted in a loss of 600 crore rupees to the exchequer. In 2018, a Rural Development and Panchayat Raj report pointed out that in just one year (FY18), 596 cases were registered against officials and middlemen. Criminal cases were filed against eighty-five middlemen, while 306 government officials were suspended and three lost their jobs in

Karnataka.[2] There is no reason for us to assume that the situation is any different in other states. It would be surprising if there were no corruption or leakage of funds away from intended recipients. It is an observed fact of life that wherever there is the possibility of accessing food or other resources, complex ecosystems evolve to take advantage of the resource. This is as true of bacteria as it is of humans. In the case of humans, the resource is often money. The only way to prevent this is to ensure there is no possibility of leakage. The present government has taken a major step in this direction by trying to open bank accounts for everyone and making payments directly into their accounts possible. This one step cuts out the possibility of money being usurped on the way to the intended recipient. There is no role left for anyone trying to influence the destination of the money.

Let us briefly summarize MGNREGA. There are about 174 million rural households in India. Out of this, only 51.1 million households got any benefit at all. The urban poor and the slum dwellers are not included in this scheme, so they automatically get nothing. The 51.1 million households, who were benefitted by the scheme, received work for an average of 45.77 days. The average daily MGNREGA wage until FY20 was below 182 rupees. The households, which did get any benefit, received an average of 8330 rupees a year. The USI scheme would give the average household of five people 30,000 rupees a year. No one will bemoan the scrapping of MGNREGA if it is replaced by the USI scheme. If any protests were to be forthcoming, it could only be from the ecosystem that thrived on the leaks in the system.

The money disbursed by MGNREGA is for unskilled manual labour. The work is usually on projects to build assets like roads, canals, ponds and wells. In reality, there are many rules about how the money may be spent. The Act stipulates a minimum wage-material ratio of 60:40.[3] This precludes the option of using sufficient steel, cement and other materials to build durable assets. The assets created through unskilled manual labour, without sufficient inputs, are mostly temporary constructions and often washed away by the first monsoon rains. As per the revised budget estimate, the money spent on MGNREGA in 2019–20 will be 71,002 crore rupees. This has now been enhanced to one lakh crore rupees for 2020–21.

There is another cost to this scheme, which is generally overlooked. It is time. The people who do manage to get some days of MGNREGA work spend time, apart from other inducements, to influence decision makers at the village level to get themselves allotted the work. Because of a lack of inputs like cement and steel, the benefits of the works carried out are often transitory in nature. No lasting assets are created and no benefit accrues to anyone. Had the money simply been given to the recipients, they would have had the money and the time to pursue other gainful activities, perhaps enriching themselves further. The USI scheme does that. It gives people money without usurping their time.

In the event of a USI scheme being implemented, and 30,000 rupees coming into the hands instalments of each household, there are many other schemes that can similarly be dismantled. The Pradhan Mantri Kisan Samman Nidhi Yojna is one of them. Under this scheme, an income of 6,000 rupees per year is provided to all farmer families across the country in three equal instalments of 2,000 rupees each, every four months. The USI scheme will give every average Indian family, including farmer families, five times the total amount, put automatically into their accounts in equal monthly instalments. Again, as in the case of MGNREGA, no one other than the people who feed off the leakages in the system or those who benefit politically from the existing state of affairs, will complain. An amount of 75,000 crore rupees has been earmarked for this scheme in the 2020 budget.

It is neither my intention nor within my capabilities to try and rewrite the union budget. I am also not familiar with the current political compulsions, which make the cancellation or continuance of any particular scheme easy or difficult. In the changed ground reality of money coming directly into individual hands, it is for the government to see where budgetary largesse can be pruned to fund a USI scheme. An excellent thumb rule would be to see whether the total monetary benefit, coming into a family currently, is more or less than the proposed accrual of 2,500 rupees per family per month coming into the hands of the average family under the USI scheme. If what an average family will get is more under the proposed scheme than it now does from the existing schemes, I cannot imagine any objection to the USI scheme, coming from the recipients, which includes nearly all of us.

Objections, however, will surely come from those who gain in any way from the administration of the old schemes. These people fall into three groups. The first are the people employed to administer the many existing schemes. Their number will decrease substantially. The USI scheme, once it is up and running after a list of citizens is ready and their individual bank accounts opened and recorded (much of which work has already been done), will require little by way of administrative inputs. About the only thing left to monitor would be to see when every citizen reaches the age of twenty-five years, so that the money starts going into the citizen's account and when the citizen passes on, so that money can be stopped being sent into that account. There would be a large number of people who would be freed up from running the old schemes, who could hopefully be employed in expediting business growth.

The second are people, who are mainly politicians, and who take credit for implementing and inheriting schemes started by their political parties, so that they can wield influence and ask for votes on that account. If any political party can muster the courage to implement the USI scheme, while dismantling the earlier leaky, patchwork of schemes, it would be an act difficult to beat. That party would be unbeatable at the hustings.

The third are people with a particular kind of a paternalistic bent of mind. These people are generally well off, who are often found in Non-Governmental Organizations (NGOs). However, they can be found anywhere, from well-intentioned policymakers to political organizations and include a myriad other individuals and social groups. What sets them apart is their firm belief that poor people are incapable of looking after themselves and their families. They believe that poor people need people such as themselves to guide them through life and teach them what is good for them. One of the core beliefs of such people is that if poor people are given any money, they will soon squander it unwisely and probably drink themselves silly. The thought that poor people, who have been forced by circumstance to manage with little money, are probably better money managers than the rest of us not so unfortunately placed, is alien to them. They refuse to accept that what keeps poor people poor is primarily lack of money and opportunities to better their lot in life. They have taken upon their shoulders, the white man's burden.

'The White Man's Burden: The United States and the Philippine Islands' is the title of a poem written by Rudyard Kipling, an ardent supporter and apologist for imperialism and colonialism. He makes it appear that by colonizing a country, the colonial powers were doing the colonized countries a favour and were sacrificing their youth for the noble purpose of bringing civilization to them. The poem was published in 1899, to urge America to colonize the Philippine islands. He describes the people of the Philippines as,

Your new-caught, sullen peoples
Half devil and half child

Our good-intentioned people who are so readily taking on the white man's burden, probably do not think of our poorer people as 'Half devil and half child', but if we are to judge by their actions, they certainly regard the poorer sections of our people as, 'half ignorant and half child'.

This group of people has, over time, been quite successful in getting many schemes passed and funded by the government. Once a giveaway scheme is started, it acquires stakeholders, from the direct beneficiaries of the scheme to the NGOs and government inspectors, who are involved in monitoring and running the scheme and to the private parties who cater to the needs of the scheme. The political parties that start a particular scheme gain a vested interest in its continuation. In time, it becomes politically difficult to discontinue the scheme. Some of the schemes acquire iconic or even sacred stature. The midday meal scheme is perhaps the most sacred of all. It would be a brave political party who attempted to abolish it. That should not prevent us from having a closer look at it.

The midday meal scheme was started in 1995. It was meant only for government and government-aided schools and not for privately run ones. The primary aim of the scheme was to encourage children to go and keep going to school. Though touted also as a scheme for providing nourishment to children, providing some nourishment was an unavoidable corollary of giving them food to go to school. It was essentially a scheme to bribe poor parents to send their children to school. How effective has it been? Not very effective, it seems. According to a study done between 2010–11 and 2015–16, across twenty Indian states by Geeta Gandhi Kingdon, professor of education and international development at the Institute of Education, London, it was found that during this period, enrolment in government schools fell by 13 million, while private schools acquired 17.5 million new students.[4] Private schools do not give midday meals. The quality of education matters more than midday meals do. About half of India's children go to private schools and that percentage is increasing. In urban India, the children going to private schools are much more than those who go to government schools. Studies in cities as diverse as Mumbai and Patna show that upwards of 75 per cent of children in these cities are attending private schools.[5]

There is definitely merit in saying that because of the midday meal scheme, children from extremely impoverished homes at least get something to eat once a day. With an average additional 2,500 rupees coming into every family every month, their situation will not be as dire as it may earlier have been. There will then be no reason for government schoolchildren not to revert to the time-honoured practice of carrying a tiffin box to school with a tasty and nutritious paratha or sandwich or whatever the parents decide, in it. It will almost certainly be more to the child's liking, than a mass-produced something given to the child. The cost of the sandwich or equivalent will be about five rupees. With an average of twenty school days a month, it will amount to 100 rupees a month. There is no valid reason for not ending the midday meal scheme, for which 11,000 crore rupees have been earmarked in the 2020 central budget, along with announcing the USI scheme. The do-gooders would have us believe that even if poor parents have the means to feed their child, they would not do so and may perhaps spend the money on alcohol.

If a near sacred scheme, like the midday meal in school scheme, can be looked at in the cold light of reason, there is no reason why other schemes too should not be re-evaluated. There are different umbrella schemes for the development of schedule castes, schedule tribes, minorities and just other vulnerable groups, each one of them being given budgets in the thousands of crores. If money were to be coming directly into the pockets of all these tribes and groups, they would be happy to develop themselves, and not really want to be any white man's burden. All the schemes designed by the tribe of do-gooders can and should be disbanded, if for no other reason than just to hand their dignity back to all these groups. All that the government, whether central or state, would need to do is ensure access to education and community health as it indeed has to for the entire country.

A small reality check on NGOs is in order. India has 3.1 million NGOs, that is one NGO for every 400 people as against one policeman for every 709 people and more than double the number of schools in the country.[6] If these NGOs were at all effective, India should already have been the proverbial land of milk and honey. Unfortunately, there is no evidence of that.

My thinking is that a large part of the 7.8 lakh crore, needed for the USI scheme every year, can be funded by trimming existing budget proposals. A small portion of the USI money will go to richer people, who do not in any way need the helping hand. We can very easily get that money back from the rich folks and a little more too, by increasing their taxes a little. If people with an annual taxable income in excess of 10 lakh rupees, are taxed an extra 5 per cent on the amount greater than 10 lakhs, it should bring an approximate additional one lakh crore into the exchequer. As the USI money will be free of all taxes and every individual will be receiving 12,000 rupees every year, only people with an annual taxable income of 12.4 lakhs a year will start having any outflow of money from their pockets. In the case of a single earner in our average family of five, which will receive 30,000 rupees every year, money outflow will start only after a taxable income of 16 lakhs is crossed. Considering that only less than 1.15 per cent of our citizens pay any taxes at all, a very small number of people will be called upon to make a small contribution to kick-starting the economy and curtail joblessness. If there is still a shortfall, deficit financing of the difference will be a worthwhile investment for the creation of tens of millions of jobs and ending untold suffering.

To the approximately 1 per cent of Indians who will contribute very partially to the funding of the scheme and who may resent the idea of giving away a little of their money and receiving nothing in return, I urge them to consider the following. We will not get anarchy. We will all get more convivial lives. If a man is hungry, no amount of deterrent laws will prevent him from stealing or worse, in order for him to feed himself and his family. If a poor man has a little money to spend and perhaps the opportunity to earn a little more, he will not be a burden upon you and will increase your own wealth a little whether directly or indirectly. We may no longer be beset by beggars at every traffic intersection or have petty thieves trying to eke out a living. We may see a diminishing of city slums as more jobs are created in the villages and small towns. We may even see a reversal of the flow of jobless people from the villages to city slums. If a man only has misery in his life, then that is what he will spread. If he has a little money, he will spread that. It is seldom that modest inputs from a few can contribute to improving the quality of life of a sixth of humanity. On the whole we will receive quite significantly for the little money we contribute.

The funding of the USI scheme need not result in a constant drain on the exchequer of the country. The tens of millions of jobs that will be created by the proposed USI plan will be because of the economic activity that it will unleash. Economic activity results in profits and taxes for the exchequer. It may be difficult for the government to garner taxes from millions of small ventures. It is time, I think, to seriously consider some carrots in addition to only a stick to induce people to pay taxes. Apart from the inflation-protected, long-term saving plan, deposits into which are linked to taxes paid by individuals that I had mentioned in the previous chapter, other carrots that may yield results can also be dangled.

We have considered the three major advantages which we have that can make a USI scheme possible, namely, a family-oriented culture, a low cost of living and a plethora of inefficient schemes which can be cannibalized to implement one potent scheme, which can, in one fell swoop, solve many of our problems. Let us now consider the one major disadvantage that India has and which again, is not shared by most other countries. It is bureaucratic control and the prevailing regimen of various permissions, licences, excessive reports and multiple departments, each with the power to delay indefinitely. This is not a recipe for job creation.

Recall Professor Moretti's research. Jobs were created everywhere, except Italy where, because of bureaucratic controls, jobs were actually lost despite new money coming into communities. It could be the same story in India, despite humongous sums of new money coming into communities. If the task of starting new ventures and businesses is too risk-prone and arduous, people who may otherwise have tried to do something will then sit back and simply try to enjoy the little extra money that is coming their way, causing no job creation but surely causing inflation. It is time we took cognizance of the reality that bureaucratic practices, as they currently are, are a millstone about our necks, and if we as a nation are to be productive and stand tall, we need to reorient the priorities of the bureaucracy.

The mindset to control things, often without any compelling rationale, perhaps from a misplaced sense of morality, was made evident when, at the start of the coronavirus-caused lockdown, liquor sales were banned. People forced to stay home may even have had a drink more than they normally did, all the while filling every state's coffers. It was a win-win situation as far as the people and the exchequer were concerned. The ban on liquor sales turned it into a lose-lose situation. When the folly of the action became apparent, the orders were rescinded, but to add insult to injury, many states greatly increased the already high rates of taxation on liquor. Moralistic stances generally deter growth.

Unless the mindset to obsessively control all activities is reversed, no amount of monetary stimulus will yield significant results. This is easier said than done. We, as a country, are so enmeshed in a tightly woven web of rules, regulations, compliances and filings, that it constricts all enterprise. First, there is a mega-web of 1,536 laws that govern doing business in India, of which 678 are enacted by Parliament and 858 by state legislative assemblies. From this web emerge mini webs of 69,233 compliances, 25,539 at the union level and 43,696 in the states. Finally, following these mega and mini webs is born a micro-web of 6,618 filings, 2,282 for the union government and 4,336 for the state governments.

This clear regulatory overreach happens across seven categories—labour, finance and taxation, environment, health and safety, secretarial, commercial, industry-specific and general. Further, these can be of twelve types—licences, registrations, permissions, consent orders, returns, displays, registers, challans, payments, remittances, renewals and notices. And as if these laws, compliances and filings across categories and types were not enough, they change at the rate of 3,000 a year. In the last quarter alone, there were 1,206 changes, or about thirteen a day.[7]

If this multitude of laws, rules and regulations is not diligently followed, or if any one of them is inadvertently skirted, one could find oneself making regular court appearances for the next few years. A system such as the one we exist in, will always take an entrepreneur's focus away from running her or his enterprise. The focus will shift from satisfying customers to not falling foul of one of the tripwires set up by the plethora of rules. This is not about killing the goose that lays golden eggs. This is killing the goose before any golden eggs can be laid.

Looking at the situation from a different viewpoint, we as Indians, have reason to rejoice. Despite being hobbled, restrained, shackled and fettered as badly as enterprise from any country has ever been, we have not done too badly. For the past few years, until the coming of the coronavirus, India's GDP has been amongst the highest growing among the countries of the world. Can we even begin to imagine how we would perform if we were freed?

To the best of my knowledge, there is no rule, notification or law against scratching your own nose. If, however, the coronavirus persists, with the perfectly valid reason of protecting you against infection, a notification will be issued against such indiscretions, which will need to be recorded and reported at prescribed intervals.

The Indian government has, since the past few years, been resolute in defending our borders against external enemies. It needs to be equally resolute in waging war against a paralysing system that has enslaved us and sucked out all initiative and enterprise from the people of the country. Without that resolve, it should forego all thoughts of a USI scheme. That would just be money down the drain.

Recently, the prime minister announced an economic stimulus of 20 lakh crores. A stimulus of this size is unprecedented and is possibly a once-in-a-lifetime opportunity, which must not be squandered. If ever there was an opportune moment for starting a USI scheme and liberating the system, it is now.

12

LIFE AFTER TECHNOLOGICAL ADVANCES AND USI

At any point of time, multiple futures are possible. The future we eventually get will depend on the steps we take or do not take today. Our present is the way it is because of steps we took or did not take in the past. We cannot undo the past but we can certainly plan for the future. Small steps can often yield profound results. The emergence of life itself depended on the abilities of random molecules to replicate themselves in the primordial soup of the early oceans. Sexual transmission of genes to the next generation, working through evolution, gave rise to the unbounded variety of life we see around us.

This process of small changes yielding large results is known as emergence. Emergence refers to the existence of collective behaviours. What parts of a system can do together, they cannot do alone. Emergent properties can be very different from the properties of the constituents of the system. Individual muscle cells give no sign of the power exhibited by a muscle when many cells join together to form a bicep or other muscle. An individual plant gives no sign of the biodiversity and ecosystem of a tropical rainforest. A water molecule has the emergent properties of oxygen and hydrogen atoms. Many water molecules together form river flows and ocean waves. Emergent structures are patterns that emerge via the collective actions of many individual entities. To explain such patterns, as did Aristotle, is that emergent structures are other than the sum of their parts.[1, 2]

This book proposes the introduction of three new variables

to the existing scheme of things. The first is a USI scheme, which will encourage spending, risk-taking and innovation. The second is tweaking the rules of bureaucracy to reward it for ventures started. The third is measures to speed up the justice delivery system, with an emphasis on contract enforcements. The book also advocates a liberal and permissive backdrop so as not to foil emergence. What will emerge from the introduction of these new factors may pleasantly surprise even the most optimistic. The interaction of these three variables with each other and the existing situation, will yield far bigger changes than if any of these variables was acting alone.

If a USI scheme is implemented, it will not only generate jobs, it will change our lives and also us in many ways. But let us consider jobs first. The entire first part of this book in which we tried to follow technological breakthroughs across many areas, we saw that one of the major consequences of these developments was going to be a loss of jobs. How can we then consider job creation, when technology is expected to progressively take over jobs that humans now do? Before we go on to see what nature of jobs we can expect to be created, that humans can perform better than machines, let us recapitulate the nature of jobs that will be lost.

The jobs that will be lost are very varied, but if we were to try and use one word to label most of them, it would be routine jobs. Whether it is factory workers, making anything from cars to sewing machines or farm workers who toil away to grow food for us, or miners extracting coal from the bowels of the earth, each of these workers produce something tangible. The truck drivers, train drivers and ship crews transporting goods or airline pilots and taxi drivers are also routine jobs not requiring much human interaction. These jobs may, to an extent, be psychologically rewarding as the people who perform the jobs have the satisfaction of knowing they are doing something worthwhile and of economic value to society. They may also enjoy the camaraderie of fellow workers. However, the actual act of performing these jobs was seldom pleasurable. They were repetitive jobs, often performed under conditions of physical discomfort. The building of cars may have a degree of glamour attached to it, but there is nothing glamorous about welding the same bits of cars together or tightening the same nuts and bolts together every day. Still these jobs put food on the table and pay the bills. It is a way of life.

If these existing jobs are lost but other jobs are available to be taken up, it would be no great loss. All existing jobs will not be lost simultaneously but would diminish over time. Certainly, for the people who have to switch from one job to another, there would be a period of unsettlement. An existing USI scheme will soften the trauma of locating a new job. New job entrants would in any case be accustomed to the new way of life and be adjusted to it from the beginning.

If technology is expected to progressively take over jobs that are currently being performed by humans, how can we then expect new jobs to be created? The answer is that there are many things which technology will not be able to do and which perhaps too few humans are now doing. Most of the new jobs will be in the service sector. We do not need to compete with machines for jobs that machines can do better than us. That would be a losing proposition. We need instead to focus on jobs in which it would be difficult for machines to compete with us. Some may think that it is a step down in life from being say, factory workers or truck drivers to working in the service industry, but that need not be the way service jobs turn out to be. Let us consider Maslow's hierarchy of needs.

The most prominent theory to explain the relationship between income and subjective well-being (SWB) is the need theory, which proposes that increased income and wealth can lead to increased SWB in poverty, because money is used to satisfy basic human physiological needs. Abraham Harold Maslow was an

American psychologist who was best known for creating Maslow's hierarchy of needs, a theory of psychological health predicated on fulfilling innate human needs in priority, culminating in self-actualization. Maslow, in his 1943 paper 'A Theory of Human Motivation', postulated a hierarchy of needs, in which the basic needs are to be satisfied first before higher needs could be addressed. He started with the basic physiological needs such as food, water and rest, the next were security and safety needs, which I understand should also include security for the future. The third level is psychological needs such as belongingness and the need for love. It is only after these are met that the two higher needs will be sought. The fourth is esteem needs and include prestige and feelings of accomplishment, and the fifth is self-actualization or achieving one's full potential, including creative activities.[3, 4]

Current blue-collar workers such as factory workers, truck drivers or miners are able to fulfil the first two needs. So, too, will workers in new service sector jobs with the help of a USI. I do not think that jobs or vocations alone can fulfil the third level of psychological needs, of belongingness and love. This level of needs can only be met through an intricate interplay between many factors, such as the structure of society, family dynamics, interaction between the sexes and many others. The fourth level of esteem is far more likely to be met through a service sector job, which almost by definition includes interaction with a greater number of people. For a factory worker, beyond appreciation of his or her work and the respect of fellow workers, there is little scope for earning esteem. The last need of self-actualization again, does not depend so much on the vocation of the person, as on the bent of mind of the individual and on her or his upbringing and life experiences. However, keep in mind that according to this well-accepted theory, this last need can only be met after the other needs have been met. Self-actualization comes after esteem. Overall, psychological needs are more likely to be met through service sector jobs than through factory jobs.

Let us now consider the jobs that automation will not be able to take over. A list of such jobs will be very long. We can subdivide such a list into three lists. In the first list will be tasks that are technically impossible for machines to do in the foreseeable future. This list will grow shorter with the increasing versatility of robotics and AI. Eventually, there will be few things that machines will not technically be able to do. They are already able to compose music and are beginning to paint pictures. In the second list will be things that while being technically feasible, will not be economically viable to automate. In the third list will be things that while being both technically feasible, and economically viable, will find no customers if machines do them. Let us look at each of these lists in some detail.

A large portion of the first list will comprise all activities that are human-to-human interactions. Take nurses, for example. A few robotic nurses have been developed but they all do only the ancillary parts of a nurse's job, like fetching things or delivering food to highly infectious patients. Some of them are even fitted with screens that allow patients to talk with doctors or family members. It will be a long time, if ever, for a machine to duplicate the comforting presence of a trained nurse. The same is true of a physiotherapist or psychologist or a masseur or masseuse.

Politician jobs are secure as are those of salespeople and marketers. The mediums of advertising will change but the messages will continue to be created by marketers. Original thinking will continue to be valued, whether it is in science, economics, philosophy or story writing or inventing things. Patent procedures will need to be simplified and speeded up to encourage creativity. Priests and other storytellers will continue to enthral. If we are able to take our tourism industry anywhere near its potential, the jobs in that sector alone, from tourist guides to all sort of accommodation and service providers will be sizable. Consultants will keep giving consultations. Tax consultants may reduce and advisers about automation increase, but the basic human need to seek advice and discuss their problems with someone knowledgeable will not decrease.

The second list, which is about tasks that are technologically feasible but economically unviable, is also long. We have read about Idli Amma, who even now during the coronavirus lockdown sells tasty hot meals for a nickel. Her total capital outlay to enable her making idlis was likely to have been about 100 USD at today's prices. There is no technical reason why robots will not be able to make idlis, but there is no way that the prices can be matched. Sensors today are very cheap, but sensors alone cannot make idlis. An idli-making contraption will need robotic arms, motors, boilers, grinders and other gadgets. Idli Amma can make idlis without electricity. The capital cost of automating the operation would be in the many tens of thousands of dollars. The idlis could not be sold at the price she sells them at. What is true of Idli Amma is true of all street foods across the world. It is technically possible for robots to do the job, but it makes no economic sense to do that.

It is not only low-end street foods, which can do without automation, so too can high-quality world famous eateries do without automation. Fergburger is a stand-alone burger shop, with no other branches. It is located in Queenstown in New Zealand's South Island. It claims to make the best burgers in the world and many who have tasted their burgers agree wholeheartedly. Within walking distance from Fergburber is an outlet of the world's largest burger chain. This outlet stays almost empty until Fergburger has sold out all their stocks by some time in the evening. Thereafter, customers start visiting that chain outlet. The chain store, with all its automated supply chains and quality control systems, is no match for a quality-conscious competitor. Going further up the value chain are gourmet chefs of Michelin star ranking. A booking at a restaurant run by them often has to be made months in advance. These restaurants are not cheap. There are enough job opportunities above and below the highly automated fast-food chains.

In an era when automated factory-made goods will be cheap and abundant, handcrafted goods will become the new status symbols. They will be the new Veblen goods. These goods will be more expensive than factory-made goods and precisely because of that, demand for them will grow. Veblen goods are a type of luxury goods for which the quantity demanded increases as the price increases in apparent contradiction of the law of demand, which says that an increase of price always reduces demand. However, the increase of price is in consonance with the law of supply and demand, which says that when supply is limited, the price will increase. Handcrafted goods will always be in limited supply. Limited edition handcrafted goods can also become collector items, which mass-produced factory-made goods can never become, no matter how well they are made.

The third list is about jobs that are technically doable and economically viable but will find few customers. This list also includes spectator activities.

Computer programs have defeated the best chess players in the world. Computers are the current chess champions of the world. I remember when, in 1972, Bobby Fischer and Boris Spassky, the top two chess players of the world battled it out for the title of 'World Chess Champion' for fifty days. The games were followed closely and newspapers the world over covered the story, game by game, often on their front pages. Bobby Fischer won the title and was feted wherever he went. If the top two chess players of today, or best chess programs, slugged it out to determine which was the best program, the match would probably last a few milliseconds and possibly earn a couple of lines in a few technical journals. People would not really be interested.

This is true of all sports. If Formula 1 races were carried out in fully automated cars, it would lose the spectator interest it now has. This is true of all sports and all entertainers. We go to watch human sportspeople or other performers, so that we can marvel at their achievements as humans, be inspired by them and even try to emulate their deeds and aspire to their levels of proficiency in that field and also in any other field. Simply put sportspeople or other performers inspire us to excel in our own fields.

The same is the case with all sorts of entertainers. There is an existential link between them as performers and us as spectators. We understand their talents and at some level, realize that we too have similar potential. It will soon be possible to create automatons with limbs dexterous enough to perform the Swan Lake ballet or a Bharatnatyam dance. Once the novelty has worn off, would any of us go to see either performance? Automatons will inspire no appreciation, no envy, no regret and no desire to improve. I also cannot imagine a joke-telling robot to have the same effect as a stand-up comedian. In the same vein, I believe that a robotically painted picture will be valued closer to a photograph than to a painting put on canvas by a human artist.

The list of jobs that robots and AI will not be able to do, for one reason or another, is virtually endless. If any one of us thinks about it for a few minutes, we will each be able to think of many such vocations that cannot be taken over by robotics effectively. I daresay that most of these jobs will be psychologically more rewarding than the repetitive jobs that will be lost in the factories, mines and farms.

The majority of jobs that will first be created will be informal jobs in small ventures started either by individuals or small start-ups. There is nothing small, however, either about the size of the market or the consequences of this job creation. The USI money coming in monthly will impart confidence and risk-taking to millions of new entrepreneurs, to try out new ideas. It is impossible to guess what new ideas millions will try out. We could well see an explosion of innovation. It is new ideas, which are the powerhouse of growth. A bureaucracy that does not stifle initiative and a legal system that swiftly delivers justice, are merely the backdrop for ideas to be tried out.

Inevitably, some ventures will not have the desired results and fold up, whereas others will be successful. Even failed ventures are better than no ventures at all. They will have instigated some economic activity at least, but more importantly, they will leave valuable lessons for the next entrepreneur trying something similar.

There will be other psychological benefits also. The poor suffer from financial insecurity arising from the demanding conditions in which they live their daily lives. The lack of confidence about a sustained inflow of income is a large component of their sense of insecurity. The continuity of livelihood is crucial to achieving any sense of feeling secure. Desperate acts of inhumanity, such as trafficking to slavery and bondage, have been traced back to the emotional craving for stability of livelihood. Even in modern times, there are many who will continue to work in jobs they profess to hate, only because they do not have the courage to disrupt what they see as their livelihood.[5] A USI scheme will give a sense of financial security to the poor and will impart courage to them, if they wish to try and change their situation in life. It will enhance their risk-taking ability and their confidence in themselves. It will go a long way in reducing the constant stress that poverty generates. Constant stress and economic deprivation are two conditions that the very poor in India constantly live with in varying degrees. These two conditions often result in depression. Severe depression at times leads to suicide. Indian women's suicide rates tell a powerful story.

Depression is a complex disease with many contributing factors, which can be either situational or physiological. Situational factors can be anything from the loss of a loved one to the loss of a job, a traumatic experience or worry regarding money or safety. Psychologists deal with these issues. Physiological factors to a large extent are determined by our DNAs, and could range from a smaller hippocampus, a brain structure embedded deep in the temporal lobe of the cerebral cortex. It is an important part of the limbic system, which regulates our emotions, learning and memory. Often depression can be caused by imbalances in brain chemistry and hormones such as there being too few serotonin receptors or an excess of cortisol, a stress hormone being produced.[6] Psychiatrists deal with these issues. Overall, the causes of depression are not yet fully understood and work is ongoing to better understand them.

While the causes of depression are not yet fully understood, the effects are better understood. One of them is suicide. Although the majority of people who have depression do not die by suicide, having depression does increase suicide risk compared to people without depression. New data on depression that has followed people over long periods of time suggests that about 2 per cent of those people ever treated for depression, in an outpatient setting, will die by suicide. Among those ever treated in an inpatient setting, the rate of death is twice as high at 4 per cent.

Another way of thinking about suicide risk and depression is to examine the lives of people who have died by suicide and see what proportion of them were depressed. From that perspective, it is estimated that about 60 per cent of people who commit suicide have had a mood disorder (for example, major depression, dysthymia which is persistent mild depression, and bipolar disorder).[7] The link between depression and suicide is strong.

Indian women commit suicide at the fourth highest rate in the world after Lesotho, Uganda and Nigeria at 14.5 suicides per 100,000 people. The depressions causing these suicides could be because of situational reasons or physiological reasons. If we compare the suicide rates of Indian women with the suicide rates of women in the other countries of South Asia namely, Afghanistan, Bangladesh, Bhutan, Nepal, Pakistan and Sri Lanka, the physiological factors should be much the same, as our gene pools are interconnected. Any major difference would be because of situational reasons. It turns out that the suicide rates of Indian women are considerably higher than in the neighbourhood. The average suicide rate for South Asian women, excluding India, is

5.83 per 100,000 people. In other words, an Indian female is two and a half times more likely to commit suicide than her other South Asian sisters.[8]

Whatever maybe the reason for women taking their own lives, I believe a monthly infusion of 1,000 rupees a month into their personal bank accounts, for them to use as they see fit, will go a long way in reducing this terrible loss of the country. It is possible that in our present paternalistic culture, women may not be allowed by their families to retain the money they have received. However, their situation will change from asking for money to having others ask them for money which is in their bank accounts.

Fewer men's lives too, especially in the poorer segments of society, will be lost to suicide.

It is not just suicides that will reduce. The entire outlook on life of our poorer citizens can change from passively accepting their fate to trying to do something about it. The psychology of even minimal economic security can be uplifting. If you are reading this book, it is safe to assume that you have not come from an impoverished background in India, where the struggle for survival itself can sometimes be arduous. I ask you to make an effort and try to understand the value of a guaranteed 1,000 rupees a month coming into the hands of every adult below the so-called poverty line.

Knowing full well that it is only the very brave or very foolish that would venture out to make predictions about human frames of mind in the future, I will cover myself with a caveat. When I speculate on the social changes that will be wrought in a new world, it is only a well-though-out speculation. We will know for sure only once it comes to be.

The evil of dowry is likely to reduce. There is also the hope that a woman will not be viewed as a liability, but as a partner making all manner of contributions to the family, as does her husband. For much the same reasons, female infanticide, which is still shamefully practised in some parts, should at least reduce, if not vanish altogether. Again, for the same reasons, the yoke of patriarchal control, prevalent in our villages, may loosen. Above all, there will be freedom from hunger, for the first time ever, for every single Indian. It will be a new world.

Brave New World is a dystopian novel, written nearly a century ago in 1931, by English author Aldous Huxley. The novel reflects the fears, anxieties and the understanding of technology of those times. The events of the Great Depression in 1931, with its mass unemployment, and the abandonment of the gold currency, persuaded Huxley that stability was the primal and ultimate need if civilization was to survive. Huxley was greatly influenced by Henry Ford and his assembly line manufacturing process with workers slotted into their workplaces to the extent that the novel opens in the world state city of London in the year 632 AF (After Ford), corresponding with 2540 AD. He imagines a world state where citizens are engineered, through artificial wombs and childhood indoctrination programmes, into predetermined classes (or castes) based on intelligence and labour. It is a depressing and completely dehumanized world run by a world government where humans are made to specifications and where 70 per cent of the women, who he calls 'freemartins' are sterile but sexually active.[9, 10] Today, Huxley's writings would be considered convoluted.

The brave new world we hope to be stepping into is the exact opposite of Huxley's. Stability is still of paramount importance, but the tools to achieve it will be provided by technological advances and a USI or similar scheme. It is a world awash in a cornucopia of robotically produced goods, plentiful jobs in the service sector and a thriving economy kept in perpetual motion with the aid of a USI scheme. Unlike Huxley's dystopian world, the coming brave new world is very much a utopian world.

The coming world will be nothing like the world has ever known. It will delink food from farmland, cars from drivers and factories from workers. For the multitudes, it will shift the needle from despondency to hope and give us the will to progress both individually and as a country.

Our own version of Cockaigne is within grasp. Of course, our version of Cockaigne will be very unlike the medieval European myth. It will be real and will be closer to Ramarajya. Possibly closer than what we can dare to hope for. Ramarajya can mean different things to different people. I will go by Mahatma Gandhi's interpretation. 'The ancient ideal of Ramarajya is undoubtedly one of true democracy in which the meanest citizen could be sure of swift justice without an elaborate and costly procedure.' He also says, 'There can be no Ramarajya in the present state of iniquitous inequalities in which a few roll in riches and the masses do not get even enough to eat.'[11]

Freedom from hunger, a speedy and affordable access to justice, and the liberty to pursue our betterment without hindrance, are lofty goals. In addition, there will be a plentitude of all sorts of goods provided by AI and robotics. I do not believe we are entitled to ask anything more from any Ramarajya or Cockaigne or any other Utopia.

ACKNOWLEDGEMENTS

I am indebted to many people for making this book possible. Right from the time the idea for writing this book occurred to me, I tossed it about among my family and a few friends, receiving encouragement to write it. I shared my progress with them and received valuable suggestions during the writing process. A special note of gratitude to my wife Vibha, who concerned herself with the readability of the book, often making me rewrite portions of it.

I must also mention those who freely gave me inputs at various stages of the book, including my sons Varun and Viraj and my friends Shankar Dey, Brigadier Sandeep Bhalla, Jayant Dhody, Dr Murali Murti and Lieutenant General Rakesh Kumar Loomba. I am grateful to Lieutenant General Loomba for inputs to help me reach the book to a few decision makers.

A special note of thanks to Dibakar Ghosh and Saswati Bora of Rupa Publications for guiding me through the publishing process and doing a wonderful job of editing the book.

ENDNOTES

(ALL WEB PAGES BELOW HAVE BEEN ACCESSED BETWEEN 25 AND 31 JULY 2020)

PREFACE

1. https://mckinsey.com/business-functions/strategy-and-corporate-finance/our-insights/economic-conditions-snapshot-june-2020-mckinsey-global-survey-results
2. https://www.downtoearth.org.in/news/economy/covid-19-400-min-jobs-lost-in-q2-2020-says-international-labour-organization-72086
3. https://www.forbes.com/sites/jemimamcevoy/2020/07/08/british-gov-will-pay-50-of-restaurant-pub-bills-to-stimulate-recovery/#2de797323f4c

CHAPTER 1: ARTIFICIAL INTELLIGENCE

1. https://www.britannica.com/technology/central-processing-unit
2. https://techterms.com/definition/gpu
3. https://geeksforgeeks.org/understanding-tensor-processing-units/
4. www.ennomotive.com/industrial-iot-sensor-prices/
5. https://www.eff.org/pages/face-recognition
6. https://aibusiness.com/document.asp?doc_id=760181
7. https://www.bloomberg.com/news/articles/2020-01-22/google-ceo-thinks-ai-is-more-profound-than-fire

CHAPTER 2: ENERGY

1. www.fi-powerweb.com/Renewable-Energy.html
2. www.renewable-energysources.com
3. https://cleantechnica.com/2019/06/30/los-angeles-8minute-solar-announce-25-year-ppa-at-under-2-cents-per-kwh/
4. www.tidalenergy.eu/scottish-tidal-energy.html
5. https://www.nationalgeographic.org/encyclopedia/hydroelectric-energy/
6. https://www.statista.com/statistics/474526/largest-hydro-power-facilities-in-the-world-by-generating-capacity/

7. https://hydropower.org/news/2018-hydropower-status-report-shows-record-rise-in-clean-electricity
8. https://e360.yale.edu/features/how-the-world-passed-acarbon-threshold-400ppm-and-why-it-matters
9. https://data.worldbank.org/indicator/eg.use.comm.fo.zs
10. https://theweek.com/articles/795716/withering-american-coal-industry
11. www.brittanica.com/technology/biofuel
12. https://www.britannica.com/science/photosynthesis/Energy-efficiency-of-photosynthesis
13. https://www.knowablemagazine.org/article/physical-world/2018/crash-stars-reveals-origins-heavy-elements
14. https://www.atlanticcouncil.org/blogs/energysource/is-powe-ever-too-cheap-to-meter/
15. https://www.e-education.psu.edu/eme801/node/530
16. https://eia.gov/analysis/studies/powerplants/capitalcost/
17. https://thebulletin.org/2014/04/the-rising-cost-of-deecommissioning-a-nuclear-power-plant/
18. https://www.geekwire.com/2019/inside-terrapower-nuclear-lab/
19. https://www.firstpost.com/business/indias-reliance-says-buys-stake-in-uss-terra-power-162673.html
20. https://www.britannica.com/technology/windmill
21. https://www.power-technology.com/features/wind-energy-by-country
22. https://www.ecowatch.com/wind-energy-could-generate-nearly-20-per cent-of-worlds-electricity-by—1881962962.html
23. https://www.brittanica.com/science/wind-power
24. https://www.vox.com/energy-and-environment/2018/3/8/17084158/wind-turbine-powe-energy-blades
25. https://europa.eu/research/infocentre/article_en.cfm?id=/research/headlines/news/article_18_08_29_en.html?infocentre&item=Infocentre&artid=49659
26. https://www.3ders.org/articles/20180427-sandias-first-3d-printed-wind-turbine-blade-mold-wins-national-technology-focus-award.html
27. https://www.energy.gov/eere/wind/videos/transforming-wind-turbine-blade-mold-manufacturing-3d-printing
28. https://www.sculpteo.com/blog/2018/05/09/3d-printing-for-energy-discover-the-3d-printed-wind-turbine/
29. https://www.ge.com/renewableenergy/wind-energy/offshore-wind/haliade-x-offshore-turbine
30. https://www.windpoweroffshore.com/article/1577816/haliade-x-uncovered-ge-aims-14mw
31. https://www.businessinsider.com/this-is-the-potential-of-solar-power-2015-9?IR=T
32. https://www.solarpowerworldonline.com/2018/nrel-reports-find-residential-and-commercial-solar-system-costs-fell-but-utility-scale-increased-this-year/

33. https://sites.lafayette.edu/egrs352-sp14-pv/technology/history-of-pv-technology/
34. https://energypost.eu/costs-of-electricity-generation-compared-beware-of-simple-metrics
35. https://www.nrel.gov/pv/assets/pdfs/best-results-cell-efficiencies.20190802.pdf
36. https://www.perovskite-info.com/perovskite-solar
37. https://nextbigfuture.com/2019/02/first-commercial-perovskite-solar-late-in-2019-and-the-road-to-moving-the-needle.html
38. https://www.solarreviews.com/blog/what-is-the-power-output-of-a-solar-panel
39. https://qz.com/1582811/the-complete-guide-to-the-battery-revolution/
40. https://qz.com/1588236/how-we-get-to-the-next-big-battery-breakthrough/
41. https://www.greentechmedia.com/articles/read/what-chance-for-innoliths-battery-second-time-around
42. https://www.zmescience.com/ecology/green-living/aluminium-fuel-for-alydro-4355423/
43. https://www.businesstoday.in/sectors/auto/nano-tech-start-up-log9-develops-a-car-that-runs-on-air-and-water/story/301753.html
44. https://www.scientificamerican.com/article/green-hydrogen-could-fill-big-gaps-in-renewable-energy/?utm_source=newsletter&utm_medium=em

CHAPTER 3: MANUFACTURING

1. https://www.forbes.com/sites/insights-intelai/2018/07/17/how-ai-builds-a-better-manufacturing-process/#3a2b54671e84
2. https://www.mckinsey.com/business-functions/operations/our-insights/automation-robotics-and-the-factory-of-the-future
3. https://www.moneyshow.com/articles/global-54115/
4. https://www.cnbc.com/2019/10/23/caterpillar-and-nasa-developing-autonomous-vehicles-to-mine-the-moon.html

CHAPTER 4: THE SHARING ECONOMY

1. https://investopedia.com/ask/answers/08/broken-window-fallacy.asp
2. https://www.theguardian.com/technology/2019/may/05/airbnb-homeless-renting-housing-accomodation-social-policy-cities-travel-leisure
3. https://www.uber.com/en-IN/newsroom/history/
4. https://jungleworks.com/hoe-task-rabbit-works-insights-into-business-revenue-model/
5. https://www.alliedmarketresearch.com/car-rental-market
6. https://www.sec.gov/spotlight/jobs-act.shtml
7. https://www.eastasiforum.org/2019/10/29/why-asia-needs-to-rethink-the-sharing-economy/

8. https://www.weforum.org/agenda/2017/06/china-sharing-economy-in-numbers/
9. https://www.caixinglobal.com/2019-03-05/chart-of-the-day-sharing-economy-grew-over-40-last-year-101387924.html

CHAPTER 5: TRANSPORT AND CONNECTIVITY

1. https://www.nbcnews.com/business-news/apple-co-founder-steve-woznaik-says-he-does-not-expect-n1071436
2. https://www.vanityfair.com/news/2019/04/elon-musk-robot-taxis-replace-uber-and-lyft
3. https://www.digitaltrends.com/cars/history-of-self-driving-cars-milestones/
4. https://macrumors.com/roundup/apple-car/
5. https://bosch.com/stories/autonomous-driving-interview-with-moritz-dechant/
6. https://www.economist.com/the-economist-explains/2018/05/29/why-ubers-self-driving-car-killed-a-pedestrian
7. https://www.marineinsight.com/marine-navigation/introduction-radar-watchkeeping/
8. https://www.theguardian.com/technology/2018/jun/19/flying-cars-why-havent-they-taken-off-yet
9. https://www.cnbc.com/2019/10/22/lilum-jet-air-taxi-completes-first-phase-of-testing.html
10. Https://usatoday.com/story/tech//2019/11/04/flying-cars-uber-boeing-and-others-say-theyre-almost-ready/4069983002/
11. https://euronews.com/living/2019/05/19/flying-cars-how-close-are-we
12. https://smithsonianmag.com/history/50-years-of-the-jetsons-why-the-show-still-matters-43459669/
13. https://www.theverge.com/2019/5/2/18518176/boeing-737-max-crash-problems-human-error-mcas-faa
14. www.bbc.com/travel/story/20130521-how-human-error-can-cause-a-plane-crash
15. https://www.gq.com/story/germanwings-flight-9525-final-moments
16. https://www.space.com/spacx-dragon-crs-19-rocket-launch-landing-success.html
17. https://www.spacex.com/webcast
18. https://spacexfleet.com/of-course-i-still-love-you
19. https://www.britannica.com/topic/SpaceX
20. https://www.spacex.com/human-spaceflight/mars/
21. https://edition.cnn/travel/article/how-long-hyperloop/index.html
22. https://www.teslarati.com/spacex-elon-musk-new-hyperloop-test-track-2020/
23. https://www.engadget.com/2017/08/04/bloomberg-elon-musk-own-hyperloop/

24. https://www.nytimes.com/2019/02/18/technology/hyperloop-virgin-vacuum-tubes.html
25. https://nbcnews.com/mach/science/elon-musks-hyperloop-dream-may-come-true-soon-ncna855041
26. https://electrek.co/2020/02/25/elon-musk-boring-company-third-generation-machine/
27. https://latimes.com/business/story/2020-10-28/spacex-starlink-internet-beta-price
28. https://www.bloomberg.com/news/articles/2019-12-20/apple-has-top-secret-team-working-on-internet-satellites
29. https://www.britannica.com/biography/Elon-Musk
30. https://www.tesla.com/gigafactory

CHAPTER 6: WATER PURIFICATION AND DESALINATION

1. https://www.weforum.org/agenda/2018/10/where-the-water-wars-of-the-future=will-be-fought
2. https://www.unwater.org/water-facts/scarcity/
3. https://sciencedirect.com/topics/eart-and-planetary-sciences/reverse-osmosis
4. https://www.amtaorg.com/wp-content/uploads/07_Membrane_Desalination_Power_Usage_Put_In_Perspective.pdf
5. www.desware.net/Energy-Requirements-Desalination-Processes.aspx
6. https://engineering.cmu.edu/news-events/news/2019/12/18-barati-farimani-desalination.html
7. https://www.chemistryworld.com/podcasts/mofs-metal-organic-frameworks/3007204.article
8. https://www.fondriest.com/news/metal-organic-frameworks-next-generation-materials-revolutionizing-water-filteration.htm
9. https://web.stanford.edu/group/Urchin/mineral.html
10. www.psicorp.comcontent/2d-metal-organic-framework-based-reverse-osmosis-membrane
11. https://www.europeanjournal.org/2018/12/10/desalination-water-for-an-increasingly-thirsty-world/
12. https://smartwatermagazine.com/blogs/carlos-cosin/evolution-rates-desalination-partii
13. https://www.advisian.com/en-gb/global-perspectives/the-cost-of-desalination
14. https://www.aquatechtrade.com/news/worlds-largest-desalination-plants/
15. https://sedac.ciesin.columbia.edu/es/papers/Coastal_Zone_Pop_Method.pdf
16. www.phschool.com/atschool/ap_misc/rubenstein_cultland/pdfs/Ch2_Issue1.pdf
17. https://www.khaleejtimes.com/news/weather/yer-round-rainfall-in-uae-likely-with-cloud-seeding

CHAPTER 7: AGRICULTURE AND MEAT PRODUCTION

1. https://earth.org/singapore-30-by-30-plan/
2. https://www.straitstimes.com/singapore/spore-sets-30-goal-for-home-grown-food-by-2030
3. https://www.greenandvibrant.com/history-of-hydroponics
4. https://www.researchgate.net/publication/318307802_Hydroponics_Aeroponics_and_Aquaponic_as_compared_with_Conventional_Farming
5. https://www.thenational.ae/uae/from-paddy-fields-to-uae-deserts-the-farmer-growing-rice-using-hydroponics-1.46990
6. https://interestingengineering.com/13-vertical-farming-innovations-that-could-revolutionize-agriculture
7. https://www.nasa.gov/vision/earth/technologies/aeroponic_plants.html
8. https://home.howstuffworks.com/lawn-garden/professional-landscaping/aquaponics1.htm
9. https://www.nytimes.com/2010/02/18/garden/aqua.html
10. https://www.basicknowledge101.com/subjects/verticalfarming.html
11. https://sciencing.com/wavelengths-of-light-that-are-most-effective-for-photosynthesis-12405703.html
12. https://sites.tufts.edu/eeseniordesignhandbook/2015/leds-technology/
13. https://aerofarms.com/story/
14. https://www.producegrower.com/article/local-roots-terrafarm-new-hires-2018
15. https://www.intechopen.com/books/recent-advances-in-plant-in-vitro-culture/plant-tissue-culture-current-status-and-opportunities
16. https://www.realagriculture.com/2018/08/automation-is-changing-modern-farming/
17. https://www.futurefarming.com/Machinery/Articles/2018/9/Hands-Free-Hectare-completes-second-harvest-328995E/
18. https://www.agriland.co.uk/farming-news/hands-free-hectare-to-expand-to-35ha-site/
19. https://www.britannica.com/nitrogen-fixation
20. https://www.economist.com/technology-quarterly/2016-06-09/factory-fresh
21. https://www.businessinsider.com15-emerging-agriculture-technologies-2014-4?IR=T
22. https://ourworldindata.org/grapher/global-meat-production
23. https://waterfootprint.org/en/water-footprint/product-water-footprint/water-footprint-crop-and-animal-products/
24. https://theguardian.com/news/2018/may/07/true-cost-of-eating-meat-environment-health-and-animal-welfare
25. https://www.fastcompany.com/90203024/this-lab-grown-beef-will-be-in-restaurants-in-3-years
26. https://qz.com/869646/lab-grown-meat-and-in-vitro-burgers-are-going-to-become-a-dinner-table-staple-says-peta/

27. https://www.sciencefocus.com/future-technology/the-artificial-meat-factory-the-science-of-your-synthetic-supper/
28. https://qz.com/1598076/the-first-cell-cultured-meat-will-cost-about-50/
29. https://techcrunch.com/2019/10/10/lab-grown-meat-could-be-on-store-shelves-by-2022-thanks-to-future-meat-technologies/
30. https://www.innovresearch.com/blogs/news/cell-culture-and-uses-for-fetal-bovine-serum
31. https://solarfoods.fi/wp-content/uploads/2019/11/Solein-Q_and-A_FULL.pdf
32. https://www.dezeen.com/2019/07/03/solein-solar-foods-design/
33. https://www.foodnavigator.com/Article/2019/07/15/Solar-Foods-makes-protein-out-of-thin-air-This-is-the-most-environmentally-friendly-food-there-is
34. https://bigthink.com/technology-innovation/protein-from-air?rebelltitem=3#rebelltitem3
35. https://www.smithsonianmag.com/smart-news/lab-grown-meat-earns-approval-be-sold-first-time-ever-180976460/

CHAPTER 8: HEALTH AND WELL-BEING

1. https://www.healthline.com/health/butterflyiq-ultrasound-iphone-cancer
2. https://www.cosumerreports.org/cro/magazine/2015/01/the-surprising-dangers-of-ct-scans-and-x-rays/index.htm
3. https://www.dicardiology.com/content/new-noninvasive-blood-gulucose-test-effective-finger-prick
4. https://www.medtechimpact.com/wearable-device-measures-cortisol-in-sweat/
5. https://www.wired.com/storyquest-to-make-robot-smell-cancer-dog/
6. https://www.wired.com/story/the-science-of-the-sniff-why-dogs-are-great-disease-detectors/
7. https://www.wired.com/story/whole-genome-sequencing-cost-200-dollars/
8. https://emerj.com/ai-sector-overviews/machine-learning-medical-diagnostics-4-current-applications/
9. https://www.theverge.com/2017/1/26/14396500/ai-skin-cancer-detection-stanford-university
10. https://www.publichealth.org/public-awareness/understanding-vaccines/vaccines-work/
11. https://modernatx.com/modernas-work-potential-vaccine-against-covid-19
12. https://statnews.com/2020/03/09/coronavirus-scientists-play-legos-with-proteins-to-build-next-gen-vaccine/
13. https://www.ncbi.nim.nih.gov/books/NBK482221/
14. https://www.livescience.com/58790-crispr-explained.html
15. https://www.nytimes.com/2019/10/28/health/crispr-genetics-antibiotic-resistance.html

16. https://www.cancerrresearch.org/immunotherapy/treatment-types/cancer-vaccines
17. https://www.mentalfloss.com/article/65118/7-body-parts-scientists-can-grow-in-petri-dish
18. https://www.futurism.com/the-byte/lab-grown-mini-brains-advanced
19. https://npr.org/sections/health-shots/2019/08/29/755410121/after-months-in-a-dish-lab-grown-mini-brains-start-making-brain-waves
20. https://www.rd.com/health/healthcare/3d-printer-body-parts/
21. https://fool.com/investing/2020/03/01/where-will-intutive-surgical-be-in-10-years.aspx
22. https://finance.yahoo.com/news/transenterix-receives-fda-clearance-first-105500629.html
23. https://sciencedirect.com/topics/materials-science/medical-implant
24. https://www.popularmechanics.com/science/health/a33220609/artificial-cartilage-gel-knee-replacements/
25. https://www.medical-device-network.com/features/future-prosthetics/
26. https://ourworldindata.org/grapher/life-expectancy
27. https://ourworldindata.org/life-expectancy
28. https://www.ncbi.nim.nih.gov/pmc/articles/PMC4328740/

CHAPTER 9: CONSEQUENCES AND COCKAIGNE

1. https://www.cnbc.com/2017/03/28/in-a-decade-many-fas-food-restaurants-will-be-automated-says-yum-brands-ceo.html
2. https://www.mashed.com/124676/things-don't-know-fast-food-employees/
3. https://www.thespruceeats.com/thermomix-tm6-review-4693221
4. https://www.deviceplus.com/trending/sewbot-in-the-clothing-manufacturing-industry/
5. https://all3dp.com/2/3d-printed-house-cost/
6. https://www.youtube.com/watch?v=wCzS2FZoB-l
7. https://www.theguardian.com/world/2015/apr/30/chinese-construction-firm-erects-57-storey-skyscraper-in-19-days
8. Bahl, Rajiv, *The Economic Reactor*, Rupa Publications India Pvt. Ltd, 2016.
9. https://sfsu.edu/~medieval/complaintlit/cokaygne.html
10. https://www.wikiwand.com/en/Cockaigne
11. https://www.discovermagazine.com/planet-earth/the-human-brain-has-been-getting-smaller-since-the-stone-age
12. https://www.npr.org/2011/01/02/132591244/our-brains-are-shrinking-are-we-getting-dumber
13. self.gutenberg.org/articles/Spiegelman%27s_Monster
14. https://en.wikipedia.org/wiki/Domestication_of_animals
15. https://www.pituary.org.uk/information/living-with-a-pituary-condition/male-hormones-and-fertility-issues/

CHAPTER 10: UNIVERSAL SUPPLEMENTARY INCOME

1. https://www.indexmundi.com/facts/india/ppp-conversion-factor
2. https://www.thehindubusinessline.com/money-and-banking/Indian-currency-most-undervalued-Big-Mac-Index/article20386148.ece
3. https://www.worldometers.info/demographics/india-demographics
4. https://archive.indiaspend.com/cover-story/india-unclear-how-many-villages-it-has-and-why-that-matters-56076
5. https://www.financialexpress.com/economy/how-many-people-in-india-actually-pay-tax-income-tax-department-clarifies-pm-modis-claim/1867332/
6. https://geo.coop/archives/LocalMultiplier/Effect1104.htm
7. https://sloanreview.mit.edu/article/the-multiplier-effect-of-innovation-jobs/
8. https://www.bancaditalia.it/pubblicazioni/altri-atti-convegeni/2012-transform-sist-produttivi/local-effects.pdf
9. https://historymatters.gmu.edu/5354/
10. https://wiredpen.com/2015/01/30/will-rogers-trickle-economics/
11. Bahl, Rajiv, *The Economic Reactor*, Rupa Publications India Pvt. Ltd, 2016.
12. https://www.downtoearth.org.in/news/economy/it-is-official-unemployment-rate-in-rural-urban-india-highest-in-47-years-64902
13. https://www.yourarticlelibrary.com/unemployment/rural-unemployment-in-india-2921-words/4820
14. https://www.theglobaleconomy.com/India/imports/
15. https://economictimes.indiatimes.com/industry/services/travel/indians-spent-rs-6.5-lakh-crore-on-travel-in-2018/articleshow/69034725.cms?from=mdr
16. Bahl, Rajiv, *The Economic Reactor*, Rupa Publications India Pvt. Ltd, 2016.
17. https://www.thehindubusinessline.com/news/sri-lanka-expects-2-fold-growth-in-indian-tourist-arrivals-this-year/article26028828.ece
18. https://www.doingbusiness.org/en/about-us/faq
19. https://economictimes.indiatimes.com/newss/economy/indicators/kolkata-bengaluru-to-be-included-in-the-world-banks-doing-business-report/articleshow/71723294.cms?from=mdr
20. https://www.doingbusiness.org/content/dam/doingBusiness/country/s/singapore/SGP.pdf
21. https://www.doingbusiness.org/content/dam/doingBusiness/country/i/india/IND.pdf
22. https://openbudgetsindia.org/dataset/law-and-justice-2020-21-budget
23. https://thewire.in/law/pending-court-cases
24. https://clc.gov.in/clc/min-wages
25. https://www.businesstoday.in/sectors/jobs/labour-law-reforms-no-one-knows-actual-size-india-informal-workforce-not-even-govt/story/364361.html
26. https://indianexpress.com/article/business/economy/states-changing-labour-laws-competition-attract-capital-analysts-6424424/
27. https://www.investopedia.com/terms/lorenz-curve.asp

28. https://science.howstuffworks.com/math-concepts/chaos-theory4.htm

CHAPTER 11: INDIA CAN AFFORD A USI SCHEME

1. https://www.cbc.ca/news/world/india-census-says-1-in-6-lives-in-unsanitary-slums-1.1403897
2. https://www.businesstoday.in/top-story/4-reasons-why-mgnrega-is-not-benefitting-workers/story/282891.html
3. https://www.thehindubusinessline.com/opinion/columns/slate/all-you-wanted-to-know-about-mgnrega/article9539721.ece
4. https://www.business-standard.com/article/current-affairs/private-schools-gain-17-mn-students-in-5-years-govt-schools-lose-13-mn-117041700073_1.html
5. ficci.in/spdocument/20385/ey-ficci-report-education.pdf
6. https://indianexpress.com/article/india/india-others/india-has-31-lakh-ngos-twice-the-number-of-schools-almost-twice-number-of-policemen/
7. https://www.news18.com/news/india/to-convert-atma-nirbhar-bharat-into-reality-pm-modi-now-needs-to-wage-a-war-2703309.html

CHAPTER 12: LIFE AFTER TECHNOLOGICAL ADVANCES AND USI

1. https://necsi.edu/emergence
2. https://www.quantamagazine.org/emergence-how-complex-wholes-emerge-from-simple-parts-20181220/
3. https://www.simplypsychology.org/maslow.html
4. https://link.springer.com/article/10.1007/s11205-010-9774-5
5. https://www.cswe/Centers-Initiatives/Initiatives/Clearinghouse-for-Economic-Well-Being/Working-Definition-of-Economic-Well-Being
6. https://www,webmd.com/depression/guide/cause#2
7. https://www.hhs.gov/answers/mental-health-and-substance-abuse/does-depression-increase-risk-of-suicide/index.html
8. http://en.wikipedia.org/wiki/list_of_countries_by_suicide_rates9. https://www.britannica.com/topic/Brave-New-World
9. https://www.enotes.com/homework-help/what-freemartins-what-symbol-they-given-143583
10. https://www.mkgandhi.org/momgandhi/chap67.htm

INDEX